T0220197

Learn Blockchain by Building One

A Concise Path to Understanding Cryptocurrencies

Daniel van Flymen

Apress®

Learn Blockchain by Building One: A Concise Path to Understanding Cryptocurrencies

Daniel van Flymen
New York, NY, USA

ISBN-13 (pbk): 978-1-4842-5170-6   ISBN-13 (electronic): 978-1-4842-5171-3
https://doi.org/10.1007/978-1-4842-5171-3

Managing Director, Apress Media LLC: Welmoed Spahr
Acquisitions Editor: Shiva Ramachandran
Development Editor: Rita Fernando
Coordinating Editor: Rita Fernando

Cover designed by eStudioCalamar

Distributed to the book trade worldwide by Springer Science+Business Media New York, 1 New York Plaza, New York, NY 10004. Phone 1-800-SPRINGER, fax (201) 348-4505, e-mail orders-ny@springer-sbm.com, or visit www.springeronline.com. Apress Media, LLC is a California LLC and the sole member (owner) is Springer Science + Business Media Finance Inc (SSBM Finance Inc). SSBM Finance Inc is a **Delaware** corporation.

For information on translations, please e-mail booktranslations@springernature.com; for reprint, paperback, or audio rights, please e-mail bookpermissions@springernature.com.

Apress titles may be purchased in bulk for academic, corporate, or promotional use. eBook versions and licenses are also available for most titles. For more information, reference our Print and eBook Bulk Sales web page at http://www.apress.com/bulk-sales.

Any source code or other supplementary material referenced by the author in this book is available to readers on GitHub via the book's product page, located at www.apress.com/978-1-4842-5170-6. For more detailed information, please visit http://www.apress.com/source-code.

Printed on acid-free paper

*Dedicated to **Joshua**, who finishes what he starts.*

Table of Contents

About the Author

 **Daniel van Flymen** is currently a Director of Engineering at Candid in New York City. As a seasoned Python veteran, he's a regular code contributor to popular open source projects and is a guest on the Software Engineering Daily podcast, having been on popular episodes such as Understanding Bitcoin Transactions and Blockchain Engineering. He frequently writes on Medium.com and has a number of popular articles, such as "Learn Blockchains by Building One" and "Learn Blockchains Using Spreadsheets"—he is passionate about increasing Bitcoin adoption because he believes it's the future.

About the Technical Reviewer

Federico Ulfo is a polyhedric software engineer and entrepreneur experienced in building high-scale API and ETL. He founded the Lightning Network NYC and the Learning Bitcoin meetups. His interests span from cryptocurrencies to economics, philosophy, gardening, and many more topics. You can reach out to him at ulfo.it.

Acknowledgments

This book is dedicated to my brother Joshua who always finishes what he starts. A major thanks to

- My friend and fellow Bitcoin educator, **Justin Moon**, for helping me clarify concepts, test code, and provide sound advice when needed.

  My friend **Federico Ulfo**, not just for the arduous task of reviewing and double-checking my work each week but also for trekking with me to countless Bitcoin and Lightning events and conferences over the last few years.

- **Rita Fernando** and **Shivangi Ramachandran** from Apress for believing in me and making this book a reality.

Introduction

Another book on blockchains? Why?

Understanding blockchains isn't easy. Or at least wasn't for me: when Bitcoin first made the news cycle, I tried to learn how it worked and discovered that there were too few resources addressed to programmers (like myself). There was always the Bitcoin reference wiki (`https://en.bitcoin.it`), but in those days, it wasn't as clearly organized as today, and although I read Satoshi's whitepaper, I didn't really understand it at first—at least not how the cryptographic parts worked.

I meandered through YouTube, completed porous tutorials, and felt the frustration of examples that didn't communicate the concepts clearly. So, I decided to try and build a blockchain myself, and document all the things I learnt along the way. In so doing, I discovered why cryptocurrencies are so hard to explain and understand; it's because you first need to define the ingredients of digital money:

- How does the money get created? (Mining)

- How does Alice send money to Bob? (Digitally signed transactions)

- Who keeps track of all these transactions and the generated money? (Everyone, via a distributed ledger)

These high-level points rely on distinct units of knowledge that must be understood before they can be combined into a set of commonly agreed-upon rules that everyone follows. And the best way to understand these disparate concepts is piece by piece—by practically using them to build your own cryptocurrency. So, I wrote this book for people who feel the same frustration that I did, and overcome it by dealing with the subject matter at a code level—that's what really gets it to stick. If you follow through, and do the same, I'm certain that at the end of this book, you'll have a solid grasp of how they work.

Setting yourself up for success

GitHub repository

The finalized code is located at https://github.com/dvf/blockchain-book. But try do the coding yourself—the code is structured in such a way that methods are stubbed out at a high level with the details being filled incrementally. This code is kept updated, and so it's handy as a north star.

Take the time to set up your development environment

Use a good IDE (integrated development environment) like Microsoft VSCode or JetBrains PyCharm. They are both free and fantastic at spotting errors in your code before you do. And it's well worth the time to set your IDE up before you begin. Spend your time worrying about blockchains and not about syntax errors in your code.

Know where to get answers

Browse and ask questions on the GitHub repository's *Issues* page. The repository has a large community following, so you're likely to meet others with similar problems. And if you encounter errors or bugs, I implore you to open an *Issue*.

Don't speak Python?

That's OK. Python is known for its legibility; it's a very easy language to transcribe. I have seen other programmers (C#, JavaScript, and Rust) do the examples in the book on the fly.

## CHAPTER 1

Getting Ready for Application Development

For the unfamiliar, Python is one of the most popular languages. It's extensively used everywhere—from academia and the sciences to large-scale web applications, like Instagram. Part of its popularity is due to the plethora of libraries, packages, and extensions available for free online as well as ease of reading due to its resemblance to pseudocode.

In this chapter we'll make sure your computer is properly set up for application development and that Python is properly installed. Then, I'll show you how to create a pragmatic Python project and how to install dependencies.

Python Versions

Python comes in two flavors: version 2 and version 3. Version 2 is no longer supported by the Python Software Foundation, but it still ships preinstalled on most operating systems because it's used by plenty of internal tools. Another complication is that different operating systems install Python in different places in the file system. These factors make setting up a development environment tricky.

© Daniel van Flymen 2020
D. van Flymen, *Learn Blockchain by Building One*,
https://doi.org/10.1007/978-1-4842-5171-3_1

We'll try navigating these obstacles by installing and using tools which help us manage Python installations.

Note   As a convention, throughout this book, we'll prefix a terminal command using the $ symbol. The output will be shown as plaintext.

Installing Python
Windows installation

Python.org contains downloadable binaries for Windows. Head over to www.python.org/downloads/windows/ and download the binary for Python 3.8.

Once downloaded, install Python 3.8, making sure to choose the options to

- Uninstall previous versions of Python.

- Install the pip (the Python package manager).

- Add Python to the PATH (allowing you to execute Python on the command line).

After installation, to confirm you've done everything correctly, open up your command line and check Python's version:

```
C:\Users\dan> python --version
3.8.3
```

macOS installation

Although macOS ships with a version of Python for internal purposes, we **don't want to modify it when we develop,** so we'll be installing a fresh version of Python using Homebrew—a tool used to help manage and install third party packages on macOS.

First, we'll need to make sure Apple's Command Line tools are installed, in your terminal:

```
$ xcode-select --install
```

You'll need to install *Homebrew*, a package installer for macOS. To install it, follow the instructions on https://brew.sh/, and ensure that Homebrew is correctly installed.

After you've installed Homebrew, let's install the latest version of Python:

```
$ brew install python
```

Once the installation completes, verify that Python has been installed correctly:

```
$ python --version

Python 3.8.3
```

Linux installation

If you're using a Debian-based version of Linux, you can install Python 3.8 using apt (or any other package manager):

```
$ sudo apt-get update
$ sudo apt-get install python3.8
```

Once the installation completes, verify that Python has been installed correctly:

```
$ python --version
Python 3.8.3
```

If you're not using a Debian-based Linux distribution, you can compile Python from the source: `www.python.org/downloads/source/`.

How Python programs run

When you install Python, you're actually installing an *interpreter*—a program that translates written Python code to instructions that your computer understands and executes. The interpreter you've installed is called CPython, a popular interpreter written in the C language.

You run a Python program by feeding it to the Python interpreter in your terminal:

```
$ python my_program.py
```

This converts your code to "computer instructions" and executes them.

How Does Your OS Know Where the Python Interpreter Is?

Your OS has a system-wide variable called PATH, containing a list of file paths to traverse when looking for programs. You can check what it's set to by running `echo $PATH` in your terminal. The Python interpreter resides in `/usr/local/bin/`. This is verified by calling `which python`.

Managing project dependencies

Every project you build is likely to use external libraries. These dependencies may be database access libraries or tools needed to parse documents or websites, but the important thing is that they're included in your project.

Managing project dependencies can be a tricky task, since different dependencies have different requirements—some dependencies require specific versions of Python, others may depend on sibling dependencies. Modern Python projects use package managers to cope with the arduous tasks of downloading, installing, and keeping up-to-date dependencies. In summary, it makes your life easier to use a package manager.

Poetry is one out of a handful of dependency managers for Python. There are other, more popular ones, like Pipenv. But after using both extensively, I've found that Poetry has a cleaner interface and is more pragmatic in its goals.

Installing Poetry

The recommended way of installing Poetry is to run the following in your terminal:

```
$ curl -sSL https://raw.githubusercontent.com/sdispater/poetry/
master/get-poetry.py |
python
```

If you run into any problems, please refer to the official documentation and installation instructions on the Poetry website: https://poetry.eustace.io/docs/

Verify that Poetry has been installed correctly by invoking it in the shell:

```
$ poetry

Poetry version 1.0.9

USAGE
  poetry [-h] [-q] [-v [<...>]] [-V] [--ansi] [--no-ansi] [-n]
  <command> [<arg1>] ... [<argN>]

ARGUMENTS
  <command>                 The   command   to   execute
  <arg>                     The arguments of the command

GLOBAL OPTIONS
  -h (--help)               Display this help message
  -q (--quiet)              Do not output any message
  -v (--verbose)            Increase the verbosity of messages:
                            "-v" for normal output, "-vv" for more
                            verbose output, and "-vvv" for debug
  -V (--version)            Display this application version
  --ansi                    Force ANSI output
  --no-ansi                 Disable ANSI output
  -n (--no-interaction)     Do not ask any interactive question

AVAILABLE   COMMANDS
  about                     Shows information about Poetry.
  add                       Adds a new dependency to pyproject.toml.
  build                     Builds a package, as a tarball and a
                            wheel by default.
  Cache                     Interacts with Poetry's cache.
  check                     Checks the validity of the pyproject.
                            toml file.
  config                    Manages configuration settings.
```

debug	Debugs various elements of Poetry.
env	Interacts with Poetry's project environments.
export	Exports the lock file to alternative formats.
help	Displays the manual of a command.
init	Creates a basic pyproject.toml file in the current directory.
install	Installs the project dependencies.
lock	Locks the project dependencies.
new	Creates a new Python project at <path>.
publish	Publishes a package to a remote repository.
remove	Removes a package from the project dependencies.
run	Runs a command in the appropriate environment.
search	Searches for packages on remote repositories.
self	Interacts with Poetry directly.
shell	Spawns a shell within the virtual environment.
show	Shows information about packages.
update	Updates the dependencies as according to the pyproject.toml file.
version	Shows the version of the project or bumps it when a valid bump rule is provided.

Creating a Python project with Poetry

Let's create a new project with Poetry:

```
poetry new my-project
```

This creates the following "standard" Python project structure in a folder called my-project:

```
.
├── README.rst
├── my_project
│   └── __init__.py
├── pyproject.toml
└── tests
    ├── __init__.py
    └── test_my_project.py
```

The most important file here is pyproject.toml which describes the project and its dependencies. It's written in a markup format called TOML:

```
[tool.poetry]
name = "my-project"
version = "0.1.0"
description = ""
authors = ["Daniel van Flymen <vanflymen@gmail.com>"]

[tool.poetry.dependencies]
python = "^3.8"

[tool.poetry.dev-dependencies]
pytest = "^5.2"

[build-system]
requires = ["poetry>=0.12"]
build-backend = "poetry.masonry.api"
```

Note that the only dependency we have right now is Python ^3.8, which indicates that your project requires *any* Python version between 3.8.0 and 4.0.0. Poetry has also added pytest as a dev dependency for running tests, but we'll get into that later.

Installing dependencies

One of the most popular Python libraries is the requests library, which allows us to make easy HTTP requests. Let's install it:

```
$ poetry add requests

Creating virtualenv my-project-py3.8 in /Users/dvf/Library/
Caches/pypoetry/virtualenvs Using version ^2.22 for requests

Updating dependencies
Resolving dependencies... (0.7s)

Writing lock file

Package  operations:  14  installs, 0 updates, 0 removals

  - Installing  more-itertools  (7.2.0)
  - Installing zipp (0.6.0)
  - Installing importlib-metadata (0.23)
  - Installing atomicwrites (1.3.0)
  - Installing attrs (19.3.0)
  - Installing certifi (2019.9.11)
  - Installing chardet (3.0.4)
  - Installing idna (2.8)
  - Installing pluggy (0.13.0)
  - Installing py (1.8.0)
  - Installing six (1.12.0)
```

```
- Installing urllib3 (1.25.6)
- Installing pytest (3.10.1)
- Installing requests (2.22.0)
```

Using the syntax `poetry add requests` caused a number of things to happen:

1. A "virtual environment" (virtualenv) was created at /Users/dvf/Library/Caches/pypoetry/ virtualenvs/my-project-py3.8. A virtualenv is a folder containing a Python interpreter and packages for your project, so as not to pollute the rest of your system.

2. The latest version of requests (2.22.0) was downloaded from Python's Package Index at https://pypi.org.

3. All the dependencies that requests depend on were downloaded too. These are called sub-dependencies.

4. All the downloaded packages were installed to your project's virtualenv.

We're now ready to begin building and interacting with our dependencies.

Activating the virtualenv

Before you can run your project, you need to activate the virtualenv. That is, tell your computer to use the Python interpreter located in the virtualenv that Poetry manages.

First, let's inspect which Python interpreter we're using:

```
$ which python

/usr/local/bin/python
```

Let's activate the virtualenv:

```
$ poetry shell

Spawning shell within /Users/dvf/Library/Caches/pypoetry/
virtualenvs/my-project-py3.8
```

And now, let's verify that the Python interpreter we're using is the one in Poetry's virtualenv:

```
$ which python

/Users/dvf/Library/Caches/pypoetry/virtualenvs/my-project-
py3.8/bin/python
```

Running into Problems?

If you're running into a problem, then you should take care to close and reopen your terminal and follow the instructions carefully from the beginning of this chapter. If you're still stuck, then there's likely an issue with your PATH variable.

I suggest carefully reading Poetry's documentation to make sure you've followed all the steps, since it's likely that the software may have changed since the publication of this book.

Example: Getting the Bitcoin price

Let's get our feet wet by creating some code that fetches the current Bitcoin spot price from an exchange.

First, create a file called current_price.py in my-project/my_project. Your folder structure should look as follows:

```
.
├── README.rst
├── my_project
│   ├── __init__.py
│   └── current_price.py
├── pyproject.toml
└── tests
    ├── __init__.py
    └── test_my_project.py
```

We'll use the requests library we just installed to get the price in US dollars. Enter the following code in current_price.py:

```
import requests

response = requests.get("https://api.coinbase.com/v2/prices/
spot?currency=USD")
print(response.text)
```

OK, save your file. Let's run it:

```
$ poetry run python my_project/current_price.py
```

```
{"data":{"base":"BTC","currency":"USD","amount":"9161.25"}}
```

In the preceding command, note the `poetry run...` part. This is a shortcut for enabling the virtualenv and running the rest of the command inside of it. Equivalently, you could enable the virtualenv by using `poetry shell` and then running the command.

If you scrutinize the output, you'll see the price as `$9161.25`.

Summary

In conclusion, we've covered

1. Installing a fresh Python 3.8 interpreter on your machine

2. Using Poetry to create and install dependencies for a new project (which we'll start doing in each chapter going forward)

3. Grabbing the latest Bitcoin price by making an API call using the `requests` library

Now that you're set up with a project structure, we're ready to dive in and start learning by doing.

CHAPTER 2

A Way to Identify Everything

If you're interested in blockchains and cryptocurrencies, then you've probably heard of hashing (or hashes). The idea of hashing is crypto-bedrock—a crucial ingredient in blockchain infrastructure. In this chapter you'll gain a working knowledge of hashing and why it's so important.

Project setup

In the spirit of learning by doing, we're going to create a new project which we'll build upon incrementally, chapter by chapter. We'll call it funcoin:

```
$ poetry new funcoin
```

Hop into the funcoin folder:

```
$ cd funcoin
```

© Daniel van Flymen 2020
D. van Flymen, *Learn Blockchain by Building One*,
https://doi.org/10.1007/978-1-4842-5171-3_2

The funcoin folder should look like this:

```
.
├── funcoin
│   └── __init__.py
├── pyproject.toml
└── tests
    ├── __init__.py
    └── test_funcoin.py
```

Project Structure   This folder structure is loosely what all modern Python projects look like. It was defined by PEP (Python Enhancement Proposal) 518. Poetry enforced this folder structure when you create a new project

---

Let's create a file for the purposes of learning this chapter; in the *project folder* funcoin, call it chapter_2.py. Your project folder should now look like this:

```
.
├── README.rst
├── funcoin
│   ├── __init__.py
│   └── chapter_2.py
├── pyproject.toml
└── tests
    ├── __init__.py
    └── test_funcoin.py
```

Hash functions

Theoretically, **hashing** is the act of identifying data. It's a special way to assign a unique, random value to any data—a sentence, photograph, spreadsheet, or downloaded program. You can think of hash functions as "identification machines"—something which assigns a value to a specific input. The input is arbitrary—it could be images, documents, files, raw bytes, numbers, anything you like—but the **output is always predictable for the same input**.

Naming Conventions   People tend to use the term **hash** both as a verb and a noun: "Check out the hash of this photo" (noun), or "Let's hash the following file" (verb). The correct term for the output of a hash function is a "digest," but "hash" has become commonplace.

Uniqueness   The second sentence earlier claims that hashes are unique and random—this is slightly false. In this book, we're dealing with a special class of hash functions called cryptographic hash functions where the computed hash is chosen from a sufficiently large enough pool of values such that two inputs sharing a value is highly improbable in our known universe. So, to rephrase the sentence: hashes are *as-good-as-you-can-practically-get-to-unique*.

Example 1: Hashing in Python

Python ships with the standard stash of popular hash functions; they are available in the hashlib library. Let's fire up Python and start playing with them.

Listing 2-1. hashing_strings.py

```python
import hashlib

# Hash functions expect bytes as input: the encode() method
turns strings to bytes
input_bytes = b"backpack"

output = hashlib.sha256(input_bytes)

# We use hexdigest() to convert bytes to hex because it's
easier to read
print(output.hexdigest())
```

What was the output that you got? It should've been:

5f00368a6ad231c3c439c4f6bc33c27014b4d35a904ff1656d74f9528636f496.

Now, try changing one of the letters in "backpack" to uppercase. Try adding a space to the end. Play around with the input each time. Have you noticed that the resulting hashes are *completely* different? Good. Then you've just discovered the *avalanche* property: **minor changes in input yield large changes in output**.

Typically, hash functions are considered **cryptographic** if they satisfy the following properties:

- **Deterministic:** The same input always yields the same hash.

- **Intractability:** It's infeasible to find the input for a given hash except by exhaustion (trying a gargantuan amount of possible inputs).

- **Collision-safety:** It's infeasible to find two different inputs which output the same hash.

- **Avalanche effect:** The smallest change in input should yield a hash so different that the new hash appears uncorrelated with the old hash.

- **Speed:** It's computationally *fast* to generate a hash.

Choice of Hash Function   Peer-to-peer blockchains make their choice of hash function known in their protocols: Bitcoin uses *double* sha256, while Ethereum uses keccak256. The important thing to know is that all of these hash functions do the same thing: they provide predictable output for a given input.

Let's recap what we've learnt so far.

Term	Explanation	Example
Hash function	A function that identifies anything you feed into it by outputting a gargantuan, random hexadecimal number. This number is *always* the same for the same input.	A cryptographic hash function such as sha256, md5, blake2b, etc.
Hash/ digest	The output of the hash function: a huge, random hexadecimal number.	The hash of the word "dan": ec4f...f1cb

Example 2: Hashing images

Here's an image of a $100 bill.

Figure 2-1. *$100 bill*

The **hash** of this image is e25641dc52387baba19751783ae4e060. Here's the same image, with a small modification.

Figure 2-2. *$100 bill (modified)*

Can you spot the modification? Maybe, maybe not. Look closer. (I made the word "STATES" singular.) But here's the interesting part; if I run this image through a hash function, the result is f4c56f530133b8de6b3b0b39a610be32. This may not seem amazing, but if you compare the two hashes, you'll notice that they are vastly different and seemingly random. I'll line them up for you:

e25641dc52387baba19751783ae4e060
f4c56f530133b8de6b3b0b39a610be32

Note   The breakthrough idea behind Bitcoin is that hashes can be used to prove that work was done by a computer—we'll be exploring this in the upcoming chapters, but for now, keep in mind that Bitcoin uses the apparent "randomness" of cryptographic hashes.

Let's try hashing our own image (or file), in Python.

Listing 2-2. hashing_files.py

```
from hashlib import sha256

file = open("my_image.jpg", "rb")
hash = sha256(file.read()).hexdigest()
file.close()

print(f"The hash of my file is: {hash}")
```

Let's go through the preceding code and explain it, line by line:

```
from hashlib import sha256
```

This line imports the sha256 hashing function from the hashlib library which is included with Python. sha256 is one of the most popular hashing functions (it's used extensively in Bitcoin).

Here, we open a file called my_image.jpg residing in the same directory as your code:

```
file = open("my_image.jpg", "rb")
```

The "rb" argument denotes that the file should be in read-only mode, and read as bytes.

```
hash = sha256(file.read()).hexdigest()
```

Then we read the opened file into our hash function, like so: sha256(file.read()), and assign the hexdigest(), that is, the output as a hex string, to a variable called hash.

Finally, we close the opened file and print the hash to the terminal.

Verifying downloaded files from the Internet   You can use the above script to verify that a downloaded file has not been tampered with by a third party. Reputable websites will advertise what the hash (sometimes called a checksum) of the file should be, so that you can verify it locally.

Analogies

If you're still in the dark, here's a real-life analogy to drive the idea home.

Imagine you're at the airport, passing through a security check, and you dump your backpack on the conveyor belt. But the conveyor belt is equipped with a special kind of scanner—a machine that X-rays your belongings and outputs a hash.

The backpack is scanned, and the scanner pops out an 8-digit hash identifying your backpack: 13371817. If your backpack and all the items in it are exactly the same, the scanner will always output the same number. But if you now decide to remove an item from your backpack, the scanner will return an entirely different number.

Irreversibility

As we've discussed, blockchains make use of **cryptographic** hash functions, which are hash functions that are extremely hard to reverse. Meaning, if we're given a hash, it's unfeasibly difficult (on a supercomputing level) to ever guess what the input was.

In the preceding example, if I gave you the hash e25641dc52387baba19751783ae4e060, you'd have an extremely difficult time guessing that it was a photograph of a $100 bill.

It's crucial important to understand this concept, as it forms the basis of what secures Bitcoin and blockchains in general. And there are many different hash functions with different properties, as we'll see later.

Example 3: Sending untamperable emails

The Problem

Alice wants to send Bob an email over an insecure channel like the open Internet. Bob isn't interested if other people can read the email, but he wants to ensure that it hasn't been tampered with. How can Bob verify that the email message hasn't been tampered with?

Note   Before we give a solution, using the hashing knowledge you've just absorbed, can you think how such a scheme may be devised?

The solution

The overall idea is for Alice and Bob to agree on a shared secret beforehand. Alic then removes the secret phrase from the message, and sends it to Bob with the hash. Bob then performs the same procedure as Alice: he appends the pre-shared secret phrase and outputs a hash. If the hash isn't the same as the one Alice sent, he'll know that the message has been tampered with.

To summarize

1. Alice and Bob both share a secret phrase S.

2. Alice then creates a hash H of the message M with the secret appended to the end of the message: H = hash(M + S).

3. Alice sends H and M to Bob (the message and the computed hash).

4. Bob checks the message integrity by calculating H himself to see if it's the same as the hash Alice advertised.

Note   This general scheme describes a range of protocols called HMAC (Hashed Message Authentication Code) and is described by IETF RFC 2104.

Let's look at an example. Before Alice and Bob begin communicating, they both agree on a secret password, bolognese. Alice formulates her email using the given scheme. Here's what it looks like when Bob receives it:

```
From: <Alice> alice@example.com
Subject: Have you heard about Bitcoin?
```

```
Hey Bob,I think you should learn about Blockchains! I've been
investing in Bitcoin and currently have exactly 12.03 BTC in my
account.
```

```
hash: 71890dc61c21370874d2a7b74064396cb613a1924f09aa06925abc7
842e6802c
```

Bob notices that Alice has included the hash in the body of the email. He strips the hash then appends the secret phrase (*bolognese*) to the body of the email and computes the hash of it. If the hash matches the included hash in the body of the email, then he can conclude that the message hasn't been tampered with (and Alice does in fact have 12.03 BTC).

It's important that Alice and Bob both know the protocol that they'll be using for verification. This includes the hash function to be used (sha256) and where to put the secret phrase in the context of the message (they agree to append it to the end), and any other data that may further secure the scheme (such as a timestamp).

Let's look at how Bob may verify Alice's message in Python.

Listing 2-3. hashing_emails.py

```python
from hashlib import sha256

secret_phrase = "bolognese"

def get_hash_with_secret_phrase(input_data, secret_phrase):
    combined = input_data + secret_phrase
    return sha256(combined.encode()).hexdigest()

email_body = "Hey Bob, I think you should learn about
Blockchains! " \
                "I've been investing in Bitcoin and currently have
                exactly 12.03 BTC in my  account."

print(get_hash_with_secret_phrase(email_body,  secret_phrase))
```

When Bob runs this code, he'll be able to verify Alice's hash.

How preventing spam led to proofs of work

Did you know that hash functions can be used to prevent email spam? The algorithm behind this idea is called a "Proof-of-Work" algorithm, and it forms the core of Bitcoin. It was invented by British cryptographer Adam Back in 1997, he called it Hashcash.

The general idea is to only accept emails whose hashes satisfy a constraint. This causes the sender of the email to perform some sort of computational work before sending an email. In other words, it becomes expensive for the sender to spam people.

But what is the constraint? Hashes are just numbers, but they are seemingly random, so we can apply any constraint we want. I could make the rule that anyone sending me an email must provide a hash of the email that is an odd number. But this wouldn't be a good constraint because a sender would have a 50% of generating an odd hash.

The Hashcash algorithm applies the constraint that a hash value must be lower than a certain number. This sounds deceivingly simple, but think about this for a moment: since cryptographic hash functions output a random number for a given input, how could we ensure that an email body hashed to a certain number? We can't. The only thing we can do is insert arbitrary data into the email body and keep trial-and-erroring until our hash satisfies the constraint.

Let's look at an example, and let's also make the constraint that the email body should hash to a number lower than 10,000.

Note   I'm using an eight-digit hash function that only outputs decimal numbers here for the sake of simplicity.

Listing 2-4. Should this email be accepted by our server?

```
from: dan@example.com
subject: Buy  Bitcoins!

Hey Ethan,I think you should buy some Bitcoins!

hash: 95119035
```

No. The hash of the body of this email is 95119035, which isn't less than 10,000. Thus, the sender has not done the work required: he must ensure that the hash of the email body satisfies the constraint.

One way the sender can do this is by inserting arbitrary data in the email body:

```
from: dan@example.com
subject: Buy  Bitcoins!

Hey Ethan, I think you should buy some Bitcoins!

s8763ASdh727212213098

hash: 00000891
```

Now we see that the hash of the body is 891, satisfying our constraint! (I've padded the hash with 0s because hexadecimal numbers are usually shown this way). Our email server will hash the body of the email and see that it is indeed 891 and will accept the email.

This is what proof of work is: the work is proven by displaying a particular hash, and the server can easily verify it. Another way to think about this scheme is that it is something that is difficult to generate but easy to verify.

Note   This is the critical idea that allows any proof-of-work blockchain to generate (or mine) money by proving unequivocally that computational work was done to everyone on the network. The energy is consumed by exploiting the seemingly random nature of cryptographic hashes!

Summary

At this point, you should be practically familiar with hashing functions and how to *hash* arbitrary data. To summarize, you should be comfortable

1. Importing the hashlib library in Python

2. Hashing any data structure or binary file in Python

3. Understanding that cryptographic hashing functions are unfeasibly difficult to reverse

Still don't get the gist of it?

That's OK. This stuff is hard. If you're still uncertain about hashing, it's worthwhile to pause here and review this chapter again until it sinks in. It's arguably the most important aspect of the blockchain data structure, and one we'll use extensively going forward.

CHAPTER 3

Blockchains

In this chapter, we'll dive headfirst into blockchains by using simple data types in Python. You'll leave this chapter with a fundamental understanding of what a blockchain is, what's inside them, and how hashes are used to make them resilient.

The concepts of the previous chapter are crucial to understanding why blockchains are considered immutable (read untamperable). We've already seen how to send untamperable emails. We'll extend those ideas to build a blockchain from the ground up and, with a clear understanding of the data structures involved, show why fraud is impossible on a blockchain.

Let's dive in.

What does a block look like?

Our blocks are simple Python dictionaries. Here's an example of what a single block may look like, in Python:

```python
block_1038 = {
    'index': 1038,
    'timestamp': "2020-02-25T08:07:42.170675",
    'data': [
        {
            'sender': "bob",
            'recipient': "alice",
            'amount': "$5",
```

© Daniel van Flymen 2020
D. van Flymen, *Learn Blockchain by Building One,*
https://doi.org/10.1007/978-1-4842-5171-3_3

```
        }
    ],
    'hash': "83b2ac5b",
    'previous_hash': "2cf24ba5f"
}
```

Each block has the preceding basic structure, but I'd like you to focus on the two last fields: hash and previous_hash. Each block contains within itself a hash of the previous one. Block 1038 contains the hash of block 1037, which contains the hash of block 1036, and so on…back to the first block—the "genesis" block.

A block can contain *any* data: files, images, transactions, records, etc. In the preceding example, our block contains a single transaction from Bob to Alice for $5. This block is similar to what most cryptocurrency blocks (like Bitcoin) look like. You may have heard people describe Ethereum as a "world computer." That's because Ethereum blocks also contain *executable code* as part of their data, instructing participants on the network to perform operations on the blockchain itself.

Immutability and the importance of hashes

The idea of a chain shouldn't be too far of a stretch—**each block contains within itself the hash of the previous block, forming a chain**. This "linking" of hashes is what gives blockchains their immutability and fraud prevention properties.

More specifically, the previous_hash field is the link between blocks to create the *chain*. If an attacker somehow corrupted an earlier block in the chain then all subsequent blocks will have change, because their hashes will be incorrect. For example, if we had to modify a single piece of data in block #1037 then the hash of #1037 would be different, and so the previous_hash value in #1038 would be different. **Thus, if a single bit, in any earlier block, were to be tampered with, the entire blockchain**

thereafter would be invalid. This is the chain nature of blockchains—they are secured by a chain of hashes using the previous_hash:

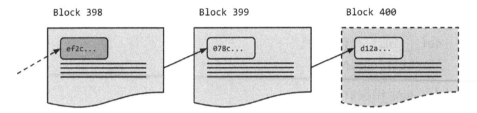

Figure 3-1. *Hashes of blocks forming a chain*

This is Bitcoin's "special sauce"—the glue that holds it all together. If somebody were to defraud a block, by changing the amount of a transaction somewhere in the chain, the previous_hash field of the next block would be different, leading to all the consequent hashes being different. And everyone in the Bitcoin network would immediately notice the discrepancy and ignore the change!

A basic blockchain in Python

Open up your favorite text editor or IDE (personally, I use PyCharm) and create a new file called blockchain.py. We'll only use a single file for now, but if you get lost, you can always refer to the source code at https://.github.com/dvf/blockchain.

Representing a blockchain using a class

We'll be creating a simple blockchain class to begin with. By the end of the book this class will be more advanced, but for now we're going to gently introduce the various concepts by adding distinct methods to our class.

Let's start by stubbing out some methods to create a blueprint:

Listing 3-1. blockchain.py

```
class Blockchain(object):
    def __init__ (self):
        self.chain = []

    def new_block(self):
        # Generates a new block and adds it to the chain
        pass

    @staticmethod
    def hash(block):
        # Hashes a Block
        pass

    def last_block(self):
        # Gets the latest block in the chain
        pass
```

Our blueprint has a constructor which creates an initial empty list chain (to store our blockchain) with an additional methods new_block, create_block, hash, and last_block to create new blocks, hash them and fetch the latest.

The idea here is that the new_block method is responsible for creating the blocks and adding them to the chain. Our Blockchain class will be responsible for all the operations necessarily for maintaining our blockchain. Let's start fleshing out some of these methods.

Supporting transactions

Later on in the book, transactions take an entire chapter. They involve a heap of cryptographic knowledge and involve digital signatures. To begin with, our blockchain will support primitive unsigned transactions—just for illustration sake—so we'll create a method called new_transaction:

Listing 3-2. blockchain.py

```python
class Blockchain(object):
    def __init__ (self):
        self.chain = []
        self.pending_transactions = []

    def new_block(self):
        # Generates a new block and adds it to the chain
        pass

    @staticmethod
    def hash(block):
        # Hashes a Block
        pass

    def last_block(self):
        # Gets the latest block in the chain
        pass

    def new_transaction(self, sender, recipient, amount):
        # Adds a new transaction to the list of pending
        transactions
        self.pending_transactions.append({
            "recipient": recipient,
            "sender": sender,
            "amount": amount,
        })
```

But for now, we'll keep our transactions simple. Later on, in Chapter 6, we'll learn more about the cryptography behind transactions, and how they're supported in production blockchains, like Bitcoin.

Adding blocks

When our Blockchain is instantiated, we'll need to seed it with a genesis block—a block with no predecessors and an index of 0. It's a special case of a block and is almost always hard-coded into software. In Bitcoin, the genesis block was created by Satoshi Nakamoto and famously contained the following text (in hex) from a front-page article of the *The Times* newspaper on 2009-01-03:

The Times 03/Jan/2009 Chancellor on brink of second bailout for banks

Now, we'll start adding some of the functionality; we'll

- Flesh out the new_block() method.

- Flesh out the hash() method (like Bitcoin, we'll use the SHA-256 hash function for hashing).

- Add the genesis block in the constructor method.

```python
1   import json
2
3   from datetime import datetime
4   from hashlib import sha256
5
6
7   class Blockchain(object):
8       def __init__ (self):
9           self.chain = []
10          self.pending_transactions = []
11
12          # Create the genesis block
13          print("Creating genesis block")
14          self.new_block()
15
16      def last_block(self):
```

```
17        # Returns the last block in the chain (if there
              are blocks)
18        return self.chain[-1] if self.chain else None
19
20    def new_block(self, previous_hash=None):
21        block = {
22            'index': len(self.chain),
23            'timestamp': datetime.utcnow().isoformat(),
24            'transactions': self.pending_transactions,
25            'previous_hash': previous_hash,
26        }
27        # Get the hash of this new block, and add it to the block
28        block_hash = self.hash(block)
29        block["hash"] = block_hash
30
31        # Reset the list of pending transactions
32        self.pending_transactions = []
33        # Add the block to the chain
34        self.chain.append(block)
35
36        print(f"Created block {block['index']}")
37        return block
38
39    @staticmethod
40    def hash(block):
41        # We ensure the dictionary is sorted or we'll have
              inconsistent hashes
42        block_string = json.dumps(block, sort_keys=True).
              encode()
43        return sha256(block_string).hexdigest()
```

At this point, you can open Python in interactive mode and start experimenting with your Blockchain class:

```
$ poetry shell
$ python -i blockchain.py
```

Instantiate the blockchain:

```
>>> bc = Blockchain()
Creating genesis  block
Created block 0
```

We should see that there's only one block in the chain—the genesis block (I've truncated the hashes for brevity):

```
>>> bc.chain
[{"index": 0, "timestamp": "2019-02-25T14:23:08.853678",
"transactions": [], "previous_hash": None, "hash":
"80ad...01bd"}]
```

Try adding a new block:

```
>>>  bc.new_block(previous_hash="80ad...01bd")
Created block 1
```

Continue playing around the blockchain.

Complete blockchain.py code

```
1   import json
2
3   from datetime import datetime
4   from hashlib import sha256
5
6
7   class Blockchain(object):
```

```
8      def __init__ (self):
9          self.chain = []
10         self.pending_transactions = []
11
12         # Create the genesis block
13         print("Creating genesis block")
14         self.new_block()
15
16     def new_block(self,  previous_hash=None):
17         block = {
18             'index': len(self.chain),
19             'timestamp': datetime.utcnow().isoformat(),
20             'transactions': self.pending_transactions,
21             'previous_hash':  previous_hash,
22         }
23
24         # Get the hash of this new block, and add it to
           the block
25         block_hash = self.hash(block)
26         block["hash"] = block_hash
27
28         # Reset the list of pending transactions
29         self.pending_transactions = []
30         # Add the block to the chain
31         self.chain.append(block)
32
33         print(f"Created block {block['index']}")
34         return block
35
36     @staticmethod
37     def hash(block):
```

```
38          # We ensure the dictionary is sorted, or we'll have
               inconsistent hashes
39          block_string = json.dumps(block, sort_keys=True).
            encode()
40          return sha256(block_string).hexdigest()
41
42     def last_block(self):
43          # Returns the last block in the chain (if there are
               blocks)
44          return self.chain[-1] if self.chain else None
```

The code should be straightforward. I've added some comments in the code to help keep it clear. Notice that when our Blockchain class is instantiated, we seed it with a *genesis* block—a block with no predecessors.

At this point, you should be wondering how people on the network agree to add new blocks to their blockchains. Since we want a completely decentralized p2p network, there needs to be a common set of rules (a protocol) which all participants follow; these are the rules of the game. Adding new blocks to a blockchain is the result of mining. Let's dive in.

CHAPTER 4

Proof of Work

The primary goal of this chapter is to clearly explain how blocks are mined in a blockchain. Indirectly, this explains how new currency comes into being, as well as how disparate people forming a network can all reach consensus (agree on the state of the blockchain). And so, you'll leave this chapter with a practical understanding of Proof of Work—the protocol which achieves this.

We'll also see that due to the peer-to-peer, decentralized nature of peer-to-peer networks, there is never one single blockchain at any given time. There are many valid chains at once, but over time, peers reach consensus on what the authoritative chain is.

In the previous chapter, we implemented the methods in our blockchain class. We also learnt how blocks are "chained" together using hashes and implemented methods to create and add new blocks. It's crucial that you have a firm grasp of hashing as this chapter is where the real magic begins—we'll be clarifying the concept of "mining" or, more formally, creating proofs of work.

Interacting with the blockchain class using iPython

A great tool to help with interacting with the Python interpreter is iPython. It adds tab completion and syntax highlighting to your Python interpreter, making interaction easier to see and understand. Install it by first enabling your virtual environment and using pip:

```
$ pip install ipython
```

© Daniel van Flymen 2020
D. van Flymen, *Learn Blockchain by Building One*,
https://doi.org/10.1007/978-1-4842-5171-3_4

Then invoke the Python interpreter:

```
$ ipython -i funcoin/examples/chapter_3/full_blockchain.py

Python 3.8.3 (default, Oct 13 2019, 18:33:25)
Type 'copyright', 'credits', or 'license' for more information.
IPython 7.12.0 -- An enhanced Interactive Python. Type '?' for
help.

In [1]:
```

Try invoking your blockchain and using tab completion on the methods:

```
In [1]: bc = Blockchain()
Creating genesis block
Created block 0

In [2]: bc.h_____
            hash
            chain
            last_block
            new_block
            pending_transactions
```

Going forward, you'll need to be proactive in playing with your blockchain class to gain an intuitive understanding of the upcoming concepts.

Introduction to proof of work

In forming Bitcoin, Satoshi Nakamoto's genius was not in creating, but rather in the amalgamation of preexisting breakthroughs by cryptographers concerned with the erosion of privacy. These breakthroughs span disparate fields and topics, such as addressing the problem of centralization and trust by leveraging peer-to-peer networks originally used to share files over the Internet (torrents); or more specifically using technology invented to combat email spam to solve the problem of "minting" money.

But Bitcoin's biggest breakthrough was the leveraging of proofs of work to form consensus among peers on a network who don't know each other, and more importantly, don't trust each other. In simpler words: in a decentralized network where everyone has an equal say, we need a way of agreeing on things; things like whether a transaction is fraudulent or if a blockchain is valid. Now, we may be jumping the gun here (we'll clarify most of these concepts soon), but it's important to zoom out and see where the different parts of the puzzle fit.

Proof of work or, more formally, a proof-of-work (POW) algorithm describes the method in which new blocks are added to a blockchain. Bitcoin and Ethereum (at present) both use proof-of-work algorithms to add new blocks to their blockchains. Proof-of-work algorithms sound pretty complicated, but in practice they're actually very simple. To get the cogs turning before we dive in, I'd like to pose a problem to you: *How do you prove to someone that you did work?*

Think about it for a minute or two. Let's say that you're digging holes in your backyard and you find a gold nugget. Is that gold nugget proof that effort was done to obtain it? I'd argue that it's proof that *someone* did *some* work. Let's switch gears here for a second—how about proof that you ran a marathon? You could probably strap a camera to your head and record the whole race, step by step. That would be sufficient, wouldn't it? Maybe, but the footage could've been modified, or someone else may have been wearing the camera. Perhaps we're grabbing at straws here, but I'm trying to draw your attention to just how difficult it is to *prove* that work was done without doubt (or trust), especially if you're behind a computer, which is pretty handy at faking things.

In lay terms, proof-of-work algorithms achieve just this—they allow you to prove that your computer did some work. More technically, proof-of-work algorithms are consensus mechanisms—if you can prove that work was done, then you can show your proof to someone else who can easily verify that it is true. There are many variants of these algorithms, but we're going to focus on a simple example to sink this in.

We've already explained that POW is the algorithm for mining new blocks. The actual method of the proof of work algorithm is simple—to discover a number which satisfies a small mathematical problem: the number must be difficult to find but easy to verify, computationally speaking, by anyone on the network. This is the core idea behind proof of work: *difficult to do, but easy to verify*. We'll look at a very simple example to help this sink in.

A trivial example of Proof of Work

Let's decide that the *hash* of some integer x multiplied by another integer y must end in 0. So, hash(x * y) = dedb2ac23dc...0. And for this simplified example, let's fix x = 5. Implementing this in Python

```
1  from hashlib import sha256
2
3
4  x = 5
5  y = 0  # We don't know what y should be yet...
6
7  while  sha256(f'{x*y}'.encode()).hexdigest()[-1] != "0":
8      y += 1
9
10 print(f'The solution is y = {y}')
```

The solution here is y = 21. Since the produced hash ends in 0

```
>>> sha256(f"{5 * 21}".encode()).hexdigest()
'1253e9373e781b7500266caa55150e08e210bc8cd8cc70d89985e
3600155e860'
```

In Bitcoin, the proof-of-work algorithm has a name; it is called *Hashcash*. And it's not too different from the preceding basic example. It's the algorithm that miners race to solve in order to create a new block. In general, the difficulty is determined by the number of zeros at the beginning of a string; the miners are then rewarded for their solution by receiving a set number of Bitcoins—in a transaction; and the network is able to easily *verify* their solution, as we did earlier.

An analogy: Jigsaw puzzles

Jigsaw puzzles are a good example of a proof-of-work algorithm, because the proof of work is in the unanimous (human) identification of an image. If we told a computer to unscramble a jigsaw puzzle

it would have to brute-force every combination

and it would keep this up forever, until we hit "stop" when we saw an image appear:

And you could now show this image to someone, and they would know beyond a doubt that work was done.

Implementing Proof of Work

Let's implement a similar algorithm for our blockchain. Our rule will be similar to the preceding example:

Find a number p that when hashed with the previous block's solution, a hash with four leading 0s is produced.

Continuing our example from the previous chapter, let's add two new methods to our Blockchain class, proof_of_work and valid_hash, for mining and validating hashes, respectively:

```python
1   import json
2
3   from datetime import datetime
4   from hashlib import sha256
5
6
7   class Blockchain(object):
8       def __init__(self):
9           self.chain = []
10          self.pending_transactions = []
11
12          # Create the genesis block
13          print("Creating genesis block")
14          self.new_block()
15
16      def new_block(self, previous_hash=None):
17          block = {
18              'index': len(self.chain),
19              'timestamp': datetime.utcnow().isoformat(),
20              'transactions': self.pending_transactions,
```

```
21              'previous_hash':  previous_hash,
22              'nonce': None,
23          }
24
25          # Get the hash of this new block, and add it to the
            block
26          block_hash = self.hash(block)
27          block["hash"] = block_hash
28
29          # Reset the list of pending transactions
30          self.pending_transactions = []
31          # Add the block to the chain
32          self.chain.append(block)
33
34          print(f"Created block {block['index']}")
35          return block
36
37      @staticmethod
38      def hash(block):
39          # We ensure the dictionary is sorted or we'll have
            inconsistent hashes
40          block_string = json.dumps(block, sort_keys=True).
            encode()
41          return sha256(block_string).hexdigest()
42
43      def last_block(self):
44          # Returns the last block in the chain (if there are
            blocks)
45          return self.chain[-1] if self.chain else None
46
```

```
47      def proof_of_work(self):
48          pass
49
50      def valid_hash(self):
51          pass
```

We've also added a new field to our block structure called nonce, which means a *nonsense* string. Think of a nonce as a once-off random number, which will be used as an important source of randomness for our blocks. For these nonces, we'll generate a random 64-bit hex number using Python's random module:

```
import random
>>> format(random.getrandbits(64), "x")
'828ad30173db207b'
```

Let's flesh out our two methods, proof_of_work and valid_hash, starting with the latter. valid_hash is simple; it needs to check if the hash of a block begins with a certain number of zeros, let's say 4:

```
@staticmethod
def valid_block(block):
    return block["hash"].startswith("0000")
```

Now, let's implement a simple proof-of-work algorithm which creates a new block and checks if it has a valid hash:

```
1   def proof_of_work(self):
2       while True:
3           new_block = self.new_block()
4           if self.valid_block(new_block):
5               break
6
7       self.chain.append(new_block)
8       print("Found a new block: ", new_block)
```

The code is self-explanatory:

1. We create a new block (which contains a random nonce).

2. Then hash the block to see if it's valid.

3. If it's valid, then we return it; else we repeat from 1. forever.

Let's add these methods to our Blockchain class:

```
1  import json
2  import random
3
4  from datetime import datetime
5  from hashlib import sha256
6
7
8  class Blockchain(object):
9      def __init__ (self):
10         self.chain = []
11         self.pending_transactions = []
12
13         # Create the genesis block
14         print("Creating genesis block")
15         self.chain.append(self.new_block())
16
17     def new_block(self):
18         block = {
19             'index': len(self.chain),
20             'timestamp': datetime.utcnow().isoformat(),
21             'transactions': self.pending_transactions,
22             'previous_hash': self.last_block["hash"] if
                   self.last_block else None,
```

```
23              'nonce': format(random.getrandbits(64), "x"),
24          }
25
26          # Get the hash of this new block, and add it to the
            block
27          block_hash = self.hash(block)
28          block["hash"] = block_hash
29
30          # Reset the list of pending transactions
31          self.pending_transactions = []
32
33          return block
34
35      @staticmethod
36      def hash(block):
37          # We ensure the dictionary is sorted, or we'll have
            inconsistent hashes
38          block_string = json.dumps(block, sort_keys=True).
            encode()
39          return sha256(block_string).hexdigest()
40
41      @property
42      def last_block(self):
43          # Returns the last block in the chain (if there are
            blocks)
44          return self.chain[-1] if self.chain else None
45
46      @staticmethod
47      def valid_block(block):
48          # Checks if a block's hash starts with 0000
49          return block["hash"].startswith("0000")
50
```

```
51      def proof_of_work(self):
52          while True:
53              new_block = self.new_block()
54              if self.valid_block(new_block):
55                  break
56
57          self.chain.append(new_block)
58          print("Found a new block: ", new_block)
```

We need to make two important deletions:

- Delete the print statement inside the new_block() method, or you'll land up with a lot of unwanted output in your console when mining.

- On line 33, inside the new_block() method, delete the line self.chain.append(block) which adds the new block to the chain (we don't want unvalidated blocks) being added.

Now it's time to fire up ipython, instantiate the Blockchain class, and let's mine some blocks:

```
In [1]: from blockchain import Blockchain

In [2]: bc = Blockchain()
Creating genesis block

In [3]: bc.proof_of_work()
Found a new block:
{
  "index": 1,
  "timestamp": "2020-02-07T04:39:03.920459",
  "transactions": [],
```

```
  "previous_hash": "1a93bd623f3e3aba2c9d4ee9193d36904382e7416b
  2fb854dbf3fc6a13cab702",
  "nonce":  "8b9991ef3ea9eb19",
  "hash": "0000075c4a6d3ae6ab06677887618cf41255d7a1ba10220bb
          3e9bc8c8ecec80e"
}

In [4]: bc.proof_of_work()
Found a new block:
{
  "index": 2,
  "timestamp": "2020-02-07T04:39:14.440383",
  "transactions": [],
  "previous_hash": "0000075c4a6d3ae6ab06677887618cf41255d7a1ba
                  10220bb3e9bc8c8ecec80e",
  "nonce": "b9a579d2cfa587b0",
  "hash": "00009d974a58fb689ad280c121897eb2f6da699db2c4bd2a3312
          dc41d478c182"
}

In [5]: bc.proof_of_work()
Found a new block:
{
  "index": 3,
  "timestamp": "2020-02-07T04:39:20.744179",
  "transactions": [],
  "previous_hash": "00009d974a58fb689ad280c121897eb2f6da699db2c
                  4bd2a3312dc41d478c182",
  "nonce":  "f4de39bb07bce043",
  "hash": "000003910a7ad733f89a9ff13ffea5b5e08fe69d581a4ecd30f
          237f95800221e"
}
```

To adjust the difficulty of our mining, we could modify the number of leading zeros. But four is sufficient. You'll find out that the addition of a single leading zero makes an exponential difference to the time required to find a solution. In Bitcoin, the difficulty is adjusted every 2016 blocks by consensus on the network. The difficulty is made harder to stave off the inevitable acceleration of hardware.

Monetary Supply

Now you have a fully functioning blockchain class that implements mining to create new blocks. This is extremely close to how mining happens in production blockchains like Bitcoin. **It's the mining algorithm which generates new Bitcoin**: a miner, when completing the mining of a block inserts a transaction from *nobody* to himself with an amount of Bitcoin that *halves* every 210,000 blocks. **This is how new Bitcoins come into existence**.

CHAPTER 5

Networking

This is a practical, technical chapter on socket programming. We'll learn how to send and receive packets of information over the Internet by building a usable networking application in the form of an online chatroom, which will help us gain some experience before diving into peer-to-peer networking.

But since this isn't a book about writing good Python, we'll throw caution to the wind, and consume the theory by trial, error, and example. Throughout this chapter, I ask that you bear with me, and focus at the 10,000-ft level instead of tiny details since this is complicated stuff. And do keep your Googling skills nearby to quench your thirst for additional clarification.

A brief moment of appreciation for the Internet

I'm regularly humbled by the Internet, especially when using it at a low level—the fact that I can open a connection in New York and send packets to my brother in South Africa, with just 180ms of latency, is nothing short of inspiring—it's amazing that it *just* works.

The resiliency of the Internet stems from the simplicity of its main protocols (something we're about to learn more about), TCP (Transfer Control Protocol) and UDP (User Datagram Protocol). Up close, they form simple, atomic rules, but when obeyed by all participants at a high

© Daniel van Flymen 2020
D. van Flymen, *Learn Blockchain by Building One*,
https://doi.org/10.1007/978-1-4842-5171-3_5

level, they create a robust, global network that we consume without much thought when we send emails, communicate over video conferences, or send Bitcoin to each other.

It's important to understand that network protocols are analogous to an onion: the Internet is formed by layers of abstraction—electrical signals coalesce into groups; and groups form patterns, which in turn are coupled into packets of data; and so on. These patterns are defined by protocols which determine what they look like and how they are used. The protocols themselves are decided by years of research culminating in open source documents called RFCs (Request for Comments) and have rich histories; I encourage you to read them. For some inspiration, here's the UDP (User Datagram Protocol) RFC defined in 1980: `https://tools.ietf.org/html/rfc768`.

Here's roughly what the networking stack looks like, in terms of layers:

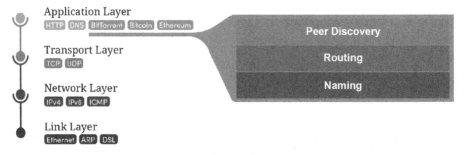

Figure 5-1. *The layers of the network stack*

- Protocols in the **application layer** are closest to a user, and logically define how users/clients communicate with a service, such as a website (HTTP).

- The **Transport Layer** encapsulates the Application Layer—the messages sent at the Application Layer are broken up into segments and packets and establish a connection (transport) between two hosts across a network.

- The **Network Layer** encapsulates the Transport Layer and abstracts the notion of a "network"—the Internet is made up of many interconnected networks, and these networks require a protocol for routing data between them.

- The **Link Layer** is responsible for the transmission of raw, unstructured data over a physical medium such as an optical cable. Using the optical cable example, it's responsible for transforming digital bits into pulses of light.

For the purposes of this chapter, we'll be focusing on the transport layer which allows us to send and receive information between two hosts over the Internet. This means we'll be making use of the two main protocols in use at the transport layer: UDP and TCP. The main difference between them is that TCP is **stateful**, meaning that a connection is established between two hosts before information flows in either direction—like a telephone call, both hosts remain connected to each other. The connection remains open until a close signal is sent.

UDP on the other hand is a **stateless** protocol, meaning that a packet of information is *fired off* to a recipient and the sender does not wait for acknowledgment; that's why UDP is often referred to as a fire-and-forget protocol—it's like sending mail to someone using the postal service but much faster.

Concurrency in Python

Network programming falls under the realm of *concurrent* programming, which is a difficult concept to grasp for a new programmer. This is because programs requiring networking usually need to do many operations at once; for example, a chat server must interact with multiple clients at once, or a Bitcoin node must communicate with multiple peers at once.

There are *many* ways to deal with concurrency, the two most popular being **threads** (multiple paths of execution within a running process) or **parallel** processes entirely. But we're going to use a different approach, called *cooperative multitasking* or commonly known simply as "async." In Python, async programming is facilitated by the **asyncio** library.

Asynchronous programming is achieved by pausing and resuming fast enough so that a program *seems* like it's running in parallel. But in reality, it's just simply rapidly switching between different commands and computing a tiny piece each before switching to another. It's kind of like dicing vegetables, except instead of completely slicing up an onion and then moving on to your potato, you slice a bit of onion and then some potato and vice versa, until both are sliced.

You may think that this affects performance, since our program is not really running in parallel, but for networking (or input/output operations), it turns out to be extremely performant and will allow our server to handle a gargantuan number of simultaneous connections at once.

Asynchronous Code vs. Threading

Writing code asynchronously is an extremely popular approach for modern web applications—the primary reasons being that you're able to write fast, stateless code with little possibility of race conditions. Node.js, for example, is written asynchronously in a single thread. Threaded code on the other hand is difficult to test and requires careful architectural planning to avoid race conditions.

A rapid introduction to asyncio

Python's **asyncio** library allows us to write asynchronous code in an easy-to-read way by giving us a ton of helper functions. These allow us to separate our code into tasks which look like they're running in parallel.

Let's get a grasp of how **asyncio** works by taking a look at a very simple program:

```
1   import asyncio
2   import time
3
4
5   async def greet(name, delay):
6       await asyncio.sleep(delay)
7       print(f'{name}: I waited {delay} seconds before saying
        "hello"')
8
9
10  async def main():
11      task_1 = syncio.create_task(greet("t1", 3))
12      task_2 = syncio.create_task(greet("t2", 2))
13      task_3 = syncio.create_task(greet("t3", 2))
14
15      start_time = time.time()
16
17      print("0.00s: Program  Start")
18
19      await task_1
20      await task_2
21      await task_3
22
```

```
23        print(f"{time.time() - start_time:.2f}s: Program End")
24
25
26  asyncio.run(main())
```

The most important parts of this program are the lines

```
1  task_1 = asyncio.create_task(greet(1))
2  task_2 = asyncio.create_task(greet(2))
3  task_3 = asyncio.create_task(greet(2))
```

which "transform" three tasks—functions with arguments—into tasks which can be executed concurrently; these are called *awaitables*, since they'll soon be "waited upon."

The following lines

```
1  await task_1
2  await task_2
3  await task_3
```

are responsible for triggering the tasks to be run using Python's await expression.

Finally, main() is called inside **asyncio**'s run() function; this tells Python that main (and the stuff within it) should be run concurrently.

When run, the program outputs the following:

```
0.00s: Program Start
t2: I waited 2 seconds before saying "hello"
t3: I waited 2 seconds before saying "hello"
t1: I waited 3 seconds before saying "hello"
3.00s: Program End
```

As shown, our tasks did indeed run concurrently; if the program ran *synchronously*, then it would've taken about 7 seconds, as each function executed sequentially.

In my introduction I mentioned that we "pause" our tasks; this is done here by the `await asyncio.sleep(...)` line within our function. Take a moment to examine this; it effectively is asking the following question: *"If the sleep delay is not reached, pause the function (await) here, and resume with something else."*

It's crucial to grasp this pattern conceptually (even if you don't fully understand it)—and try it out yourself—because it forms the pattern of most asynchronous programs. The `main` function is sometimes called the *entrypoint* to our program, and we'll use it extensively as we build.

A full treatise of **asyncio** is well beyond the scope of this book, and for the context of building blockchains, it's both important and unimportant. It's important to understand what's going on under the hood (if you care about building production-ready applications), but it's also unimportant in the context of learning about blockchains and networking because it's really an implementation detail that we can learn more about later.

Building a chat server from the ground up

Since building a blockchain is pretty useless unless it's connected to other clients over a network, we're going to start with something similar and a bit a chat server that allows many connected clients to chat with each other at once. You can even use it to host your own chat server and have friends from all over the world connect to it. We'll do this in about 100 lines of Python.

I grew up using IRC (Internet Relay Chat) in the late 90s. It's a robust chat protocol from the early internet that allowed people from all over the world to chat in chatrooms. In fact, the #bitcoin channel on the freenode network is still heavily in use today—it's where all the core contributors chat. But implementing the IRC protocol is a pretty tall order, and because this is "learning by doing", we're going to ignore all prior work and in the name of time and simplicity focus on a minimal example to help get the gist of writing asynchronous TCP server-client applications in Python.

Modern web applications are scalable and concurrent, so it's important to understand how asynchronous code is written to avoid common pitfalls.

In order to accomplish our goal, we're going to be building our chat server using TCP sockets. Python makes it easy to work with them. In fact, the **asyncio** module provides a lot of functionality out the box.

We'll begin with as simple as it gets—a plain "echo" server that simply sends back any message sent to it.

```
1   import asyncio
2
3
4   async def handle_connection(reader, writer):
5       writer.write("Hello new user, type something...\n".
         encode())
6
7       data = await reader.readuntil(b"\n")
8
9       writer.write("You sent: ".encode() + data)
10      await writer.drain()
11
12      # Let's close the connection and clean up
13      writer.close()
14      await writer.wait_closed()
15
16
17  async def main():
18      server = await asyncio.start_server(handle_
         connection,  "0.0.0.0", 8888)
19
20      async with server:
21          await server.serve_forever()
22
```

```
23
24  asyncio.run(main())
```

Before we dissect the code, let's run this server and send it some information to get a sense of expectation. Open up two terminals, and put them side by side.

In the first terminal, run the preceding code:

```
$ python my_server.py
```

And in the second terminal, connect to the server using nc

```
nc 127.0.0.1 8888
```

or telnet if you're on Windows:

```
telnet 127.0.0.1 8888
```

A Note on Different OSes

Both nc (netcat) and telnet are programs which allow you to open up socket connections to remote hosts. Since I'm not sure which operating system you're using, I'll leave it to you to figure out which to use (or install one if necessary).

Type a message, and hit enter; you should see the following output:

```
nc 127.0.0.1 8888

Hello new user, type something...
hey fellow  blockchain  enthusiast!
You sent: hey fellow blockchain enthusiast!
```

If you see this message, great—you're able to connect to our server on the IP address 127.0.0.1 (which is a special IP address referring to your own computer) and port 8888 (a port we chose). If you're on a local network, you can try connecting to your server from another computer; just substitute 127.0.01 with your local IP address.

Stuck? Make Sure You Aren't Before Continuing

If you aren't getting the preceding output, then you'll need to fix the situation before continuing. Make sure that your Python server code is indeed running and that no other process is using port 8888.

In the preceding code, the server is initialized (line 18) with a *callback function*, handle_connection to handle new connections. The handle_connection function implicitly receives a reader and writer as arguments (line 4), representing the underlying connection. On line 24, we tell the server to start and never stop.

Supporting Multiple Connections

Since we're using asyncio, try opening up multiple terminals and connect to your server. You'll find that since our code is asynchronous, we can support plenty of concurrent connections. How many? The maximum number of theoretical clients is the maximum number of ports your operating system is able to assign; on most systems, this is approximately 65,536 (or 2^{16}), but you'll likely be limited by memory and CPU overhead far before you reach that many.

Building the chat server

We'll accomplish the chat server by first establishing a simple communication *protocol* for chatting on our server:

- When a user connects, they should be prompted for their *nickname*.

- When a user connects, their arrival should be broadcast to every connected user (except themselves).

- If a user sends any message, their message is broadcast to every connected user (except themselves).

- If a user sends the message /list, they should see a list of all connected users.

- If a user sends the message /quit, they should be disconnected, and a message saying "<nickname> has quit" should be broadcast to all connected users.

Let's create a ConnectionPool class to manage the "pool" of connected clients and house the logic for the protocol mentioned. To do this, we'll create some placeholders for the methods (I've added some annotations to explain what each method should do).

```
1   import asyncio
2
3
4   class ConnectionPool:
5       def __init__(self):
6           self.connection_pool = set()
7
8       def send_welcome_message(self, writer):
9           """
10          Sends a welcome message to a newly connected client
11          """
12          pass
13
14      def broadcast(self, writer, message):
15          """
16          Broadcasts a general message to the entire pool
17          """
18          pass
19
```

```
20      def broadcast_user_join(self, writer):
21          """
22          Calls the broadcast method with a "user joining"
            message
23          """
24          pass
25
26      def broadcast_user_quit(self, writer):
27          """
28          Calls the broadcast method with a "user quitting"
            message
29          """
30          pass
31
32      def broadcast_new_message(self, writer, message):
33          """
34          Calls the broadcast method with a user's chat message
35          """
36          pass
37
38      def list_users(self,writer):
39          """
40          Lists all the users in the pool
41          """
42          pass
43
44      def add_new_user_to_pool(self,writer):
45          """
46          Adds a new user to our existing pool
47          """
48          self.connection_pool.add(writer)
49
```

```
50      def remove_user_from_pool(self, writer):
51          """
52          Removes an existing user from our pool
53          """
54          self.connection_pool.remove(writer)
55
56
57  async def handle_connection(reader, writer):
58      writer.write("Hello new user, type something...\n".
        encode())
59
60      data = await reader.readuntil(b"\n")
61
62      writer.write("You sent: ".encode() + data)
63      await writer.drain()
64
65      # Let's close the connection and clean up
66      writer.close()
67      await writer.wait_closed()
68
69
70  async def main():
71      server = await asyncio.start_server(handle_connection,
        "0.0.0.0", 8888)
72
73      async with server:
74          await server.serve_forever()
75
76
77  connection_pool = ConnectionPool()
78  asyncio.run(main())
```

For those unfamiliar with asyncio, you may be somewhat confused by the architecture of our ConnectionPool class. It's instantiated only once, and its methods accept an argument called writer. This writer argument is an instance of a StreamWriter—an asyncio object that is responsible for writing to an underlying connection: the connected user. It is handled "concurrently" because for each new connection, our handle_connection is given a new instance of writer. Think of writer as the connected user.

Take a moment to examine these method stubs, and think about how we can begin filling them out—it's simpler than it may seem. We'll start by doing two things:

1. Collecting the user's nickname

2. Filling out the send_welcome_message() method

```python
1   import asyncio
2   from textwrap import dedent
3
4
5   class ConnectionPool:
6       def __init__(self):
7           self.connection_pool = set()
8
9       def send_welcome_message(self, writer):
10          message = dedent(f"""
11          ===
12          ( Welcome {writer.nickname}!
13
14          There are {len(self.connection_pool) - 1} user(s)
            here beside you
15          ===
16          """)
17
```

```
18          writer.write(f"{message}\n".encode())
19
20      def broadcast(self, writer, message):
21          pass
22
23      def broadcast_user_join(self, writer):
24          pass
25
26      def broadcast_user_quit(self, writer):
27          pass
28
29      def broadcast_new_message(self, writer, message):
30          pass
31
32      def list_users(self, writer):
33          pass
34
35      def add_new_user_to_pool(self, writer):
36          self.connection_pool.add(writer)
37
38      def remove_user_from_pool(self, writer):
39          self.connection_pool.remove(writer)
40
41
42  async def handle_connection(reader, writer):
43      # Get a nickname for the new client
44      writer.write("> Choose your nickname: ".encode())
45
46      response = await reader.readuntil(b"\n")
47      writer.nickname = response.decode().strip()
48
```

```
49          connection_pool.add_new_user_to_pool(writer)
50          connection_pool.send_welcome_message(writer)
51          await writer.drain()
52
53          # Let's close the connection and clean up
54          writer.close()
55          await writer.wait_closed()
56
57
58  async def main():
59          server = await asyncio.start_server(handle_connection,
            "0.0.0.0", 8888)
60
61          async with server:
62                  await server.serve_forever()
63
64
65  connection_pool = ConnectionPool()
66  asyncio.run(main())
```

We collect the user's nickname in lines 67–71 and save it as an attribute on the writer object on line 72. Take special care to note how we "read until" a new line character is written by a user on line 71.

Next, we broadcast a welcome message on lines 10–19.

At this point, you should run the server and connect to it to ensure you receive the welcome message. In fact, it's handy to run the server after each change to make debugging easier.

The following code fills out the rest of the methods and completes the server:

```
1  import asyncio
2  from textwrap import dedent
3
```

```
 4
 5  class ConnectionPool:
 6      def __init__(self):
 7          self.connection_pool = set()
 8
 9      def send_welcome_message(self, writer):
10          message = dedent(f"""
11          ===
12          Welcome {writer.nickname}!
13
14          There are {len(self.connection_pool) - 1} user(s)
            here beside you
15
16          Help:
17           - Type anything to chat
18           - /list will list all the connected users
19           - /quit will disconnect you
20          ===
21          """)
22
23          writer.write(f"{message}\n".encode())
24
25      def broadcast(self, writer, message):
26          for user in self.connection_pool:
27              if user != writer:
28                  # We don't need to also broadcast to the
                    user sending the message
29                  user.write(f"{message}\n".encode())
30
31      def broadcast_user_join(self, writer):
32          self.broadcast(writer, f"{writer.nickname} just
            joined")
```

```
33
34      def broadcast_user_quit(self, writer):
35          self.broadcast(writer, f"{writer.nickname}
            just quit")
36
37      def broadcast_new_message(self, writer, message):
38          self.broadcast(writer, f"[{writer.nickname}]
            {message}")
39
40      def list_users(self,  writer):
41          message = "===\n"
42          message += "Currently connected users:"
43          for user in self.connection_pool:
44              if user == writer:
45                  message += f"\n - {user.nickname} (you)"
46              else:
47                  message += f"\n - {user.nickname}"
48
49          message += "\n==="
50          writer.write(f"{message}\n".encode())
51
52      def add_new_user_to_pool(self, writer):
53          self.connection_pool.add(writer)
54
55      def remove_user_from_pool(self, writer):
56          self.connection_pool.remove(writer)
57
58
59  async def handle_connection(reader, writer):
60      # Get a nickname for the new client
61      writer.write("> Choose  your  nickname: ".encode())
62
```

72

```
63        response = await reader.readuntil(b"\n")
64        writer.nickname = response.decode().strip()
65
66        connection_pool.add_new_user_to_pool(writer)
67        connection_pool.send_welcome_message(writer)
68        await writer.drain()
69
70        # Let's close the connection and clean up
71        writer.close()
72        await writer.wait_closed()
73
74
75   async def main():
76        server = await  asyncio.start_server(handle_connection,
          "0.0.0.0", 8888)
77
78        async with server:
79            await server.serve_forever()
80
81
82   connection_pool = ConnectionPool()
83   asyncio.run(main())
```

Let's try connecting to our server and make sure it's working as expected. First, make sure you're running the server with the latest additions to the code. Now, open up a terminal window and connect using nc (or telnet):

```
nc 127.0.0.1 8888
```

```
> Choose your nickname: blockchain_dan
```

```
===
```

```
Welcome  blockchain_dan!

There are 0 user(s) here beside you

Help:

 - Type anything to chat
 - /list will list all the connected users
 - /quit will disconnect you
===
```

As expected, after connecting, the server prompts us for our nickname ("blockchain_dan") and shows us the welcome message, then disconnects us. It's time to introduce a loop with some logic to keep the user connected:

```
1   import asyncio
2   from textwrap import dedent
3
4
5   class ConnectionPool:
6       def __init__(self):
7           self.connection_pool = set()
8
9       def send_welcome_message(self, writer):
10          message = dedent(f"""
11          ===
12          ( Welcome {writer.nickname}!
13
14          There are {len(self.connection_pool) - 1} user(s)
            here beside you
15
16          Help:
17           - Type anything to chat
18           - /list will list all the connected users
```

```
19              - /quit will disconnect you
20          ===
21          """)
22
23          writer.write(f"{message}\n".encode())
24
25      def broadcast(self, writer, message):
26          for user in self.connection_pool:
27              if user != writer:
28                  # We don't need to also broadcast to the
                        user sending the message
29                  user.write(f"{message}\n".encode())
30
31      def broadcast_user_join(self, writer):
32          self.broadcast(writer, f"{writer.nickname}
            just joined")
33
34      def broadcast_user_quit(self, writer):
35          self.broadcast(writer, f"{writer.nickname}
            just quit")
36
37      def broadcast_new_message(self, writer, message):
38          self.broadcast(writer, f"[{writer.nickname}]
            {message}")
39
40      def list_users(self,  writer):
41          message = "===\n"
42          message += "Currently connected users:"
43          for user in self.connection_pool:
44              if user == writer:
45                  message += f"\n - {user.nickname} (you)"
46              else:
```

```
47                     message += f"\n - {user.nickname}"
48
49          message += "\n==="
50          writer.write(f"{message}\n".encode())
51
52      def add_new_user_to_pool(self, writer):
53          self.connection_pool.add(writer)
54
55      def remove_user_from_pool(self, writer):
56          self.connection_pool.remove(writer)
57
58
59  async def handle_connection(reader, writer):
60      # Get a nickname for the new client
61      writer.write("> Choose your nickname: ".encode())
62
63      response = await reader.readuntil(b"\n")
64      writer.nickname = response.decode().strip()
65
66      connection_pool.add_new_user_to_pool(writer)
67      connection_pool.send_welcome_message(writer)
68
69      # Announce the arrival of this new user
70      connection_pool.broadcast_user_join(writer)
71
72      while True:
73          try:
74              data = await reader.readuntil(b"\n")
75          except asyncio.exceptions.IncompleteReadError:
76              connection_pool.broadcast_user_quit(writer)
77              break
78
```

```
79          message = data.decode().strip()
80          if message == "/quit":
81              connection_pool.broadcast_user_quit(writer)
82              break
83          elif message == "/list":
84              connection_pool.list_users(writer)
85          else:
86              connection_pool.broadcast_new_message
                (writer, message)
87
88          await writer.drain()
89
90          if writer.is_closing():
91              break
92
93      # We're now outside the message loop, and the user has
            quit. Let's clean up...
94      writer.close()
95      await writer.wait_closed()
96      connection_pool.remove_user_from_pool(writer)
97
98
99  async def main():
100     server = await asyncio.start_server(handle_
        connection, "0.0.0.0", 8888)
101
102     async with server:
103         await server.serve_forever()
104
105
106 connection_pool = ConnectionPool()
107 asyncio.run(main())
```

We introduce the loop on lines 72–91. Notice how we wrap user input (line 74) in a try-except block to cater for a user whose connection drops without notice. We then continue processing their message—checking if it's a quit or list method—until we again await further input.

At this point our chat server is fully functional. Let's open up two or three terminals to simulate a real chat room:

Figure 5-2. *Two terminals, side by side, simulating two users chatting with each other*

Note   Get a friend to connect to your server on your local network by giving them the IP address of your computer. You could also host your chat server with a web host and give it a fully qualified URL for any user on the Internet to connect to.

It's important to experiment and play with the concepts demonstrated in this walk-through as they'll play a crucial role in the goal of this book: the foundational network layer for our blockchain network.

> Tip   The full source code is located on the GitHub repository at
> https://github.com/dvf/blockchain-book.

Protocols

Protocols are extremely important in the design of p2p networks. Protocols are the "rules of the game," and they're difficult to design because they require long-term foresight and planning. A lack of sound architecture produces architectural rifts down the road—problems which require so-called "hard forks"; or a change in the underlying protocol of the network. Good planning leaves ample room for future impacts, be they technological advances or societal changes in the network.

Part of Bitcoin's success is the simplicity of its protocol and the careful consideration of its core developers when making new changes. Rifts at the protocol level have often resulted in community-driven "hard forks" such as Bitcoin Cash and the myriad of spin-off branches of Bitcoin's blockchain. It's interesting to study why and when these forks happened because they're almost always the result of disagreements at the protocol level.

With that in mind, let's look at the chat server that we've built and dissect its protocol by looking at the "messages" possible. It's helpful to break these down into "user stories":

- As a connected user, I may quit by sending the message /quit.

- As a connected user, I may list all connected users by sending the message /list.

- As a connected user, any text (excluding the mentioned messages) that I send is broadcast to all connected clients.

Our toy chat server is extraordinarily simple. But by defining the preceding protocol, we're able to make it *generic*; this is crucial because it means that *any* client on the Internet, using their own software, only needs to obey the protocol to successfully engage with our server.

By implementing Bitcoin's protocol, developers are able to write their own software to interact with the network. They only need to see what kinds of stories and messages are possible on the network. The Bitcoin Wiki faithfully serves this information, here: `https://en.bitcoin.it/ wiki/Protocol_documentation`. When you download the software called "Bitcoin Core," you're really downloading the *reference* implementation of the protocol, designed and maintained by developers who devote their free time to Bitcoin.

Groundwork for building a blockchain

Peer-to-peer networks are made possible by every client on the network collectively implementing the decided protocol. As an exercise, pause for a moment and try to figure out what messages should be possible in a peer-to-peer network.

Following the advice, it's helpful to first break our network into user stories to help clarify what messages are needed. Let's define the notion of *connected* node to mean a node amply connected to enough other peers to form a network. Here are some possible stories:

- As a *node*, I'm able to connect to peers by discovering them*.

- As a *connected node*, I'm able to publish a list of my peers to anyone requesting them.

- As a *connected node*, I'm able to accept and broadcast a new transaction from a peer.

- As a *connected node*, I'm able to server the contents of a block to any peer requesting it.

- As a *connected node*, I'm able to accept a new block and add it to my blockchain if it meets certain criteria.

Gossip

The preceding list isn't exhaustive by any means—we haven't taken into account punitive measures for peers who misbehave or formed any sort of resolution when two valid (conflicting) blocks need to be added—but for now this is a good basis to build on. But most importantly, since there is no central authority, we need a way for a peer to localize the network and form a *swarm*.

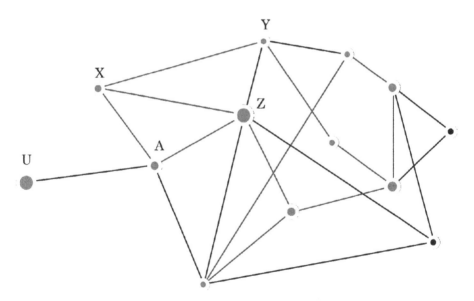

Figure 5-3. *A node joining a network for the first time*

In the preceding image, a node U must acquire a list of other nodes (peers) from A, and A in turn has acquired a list of nodes from his neighbors, X, Y, and Z, and must continually "heartbeat" them in order to make sure they're still "alive" on the network. A must also announce U's presence to the network and so on and so forth. This general scheme is called a gossip protocol, and a successful gossip protocol is what makes for a resilient, decentralized network.

CHAPTER 6

Cryptography 101

The study of the algorithms presented in this chapter are well beyond the scope of any book you can find or course you can take. They require years of understanding and treatment and build upon algebraic concepts familiar to specific fields of mathematics. But luckily theoretical insight into how cryptographic algorithms work isn't a requirement for using these tools in practice, so long as you understand their purpose and implications. In other words, a working knowledge of how to use cryptographic libraries is what's important here.

If you're like me (not a cryptographer), the correct approach to this material is that of caution. I understand just enough cryptography to know that it's a lifelong balance—a study of trade-offs between security, convenience, and speed—with shifting attack vectors as technology improves. As somebody learning this stuff for the first time, you should err on the side of battle-tested, well-known best practices and tools. There's far too much at stake in our digital world to take shortcuts—the majority of breaches and attacks on the Internet are caused by simple mistakes: using bad implementations of things not quite understood or, even worse, personal stamps of approval. There's an adage in the cryptography world: *never roll your own brand of cryptography*.

Cryptography is the *crypto* in cryptocurrency. And real cryptographers can get annoyed at the usage of the word *crypto* to mean cryptocurrency. Signing a check in real life is very similar to signing a blockchain transaction—but it's even more secure, because the signature cannot be forged. In fact, it changes depending on the document you're signing!

© Daniel van Flymen 2020
D. van Flymen, *Learn Blockchain by Building One*,
https://doi.org/10.1007/978-1-4842-5171-3_6

Sending messages with integrity

Before we dive into digital signatures and public key cryptography, I want to draw on your knowledge of hashing by showing you how they can be used to send unforgeable messages over an insecure medium, like the Internet.

Note   Note that this example is just a toy example and there are well-built libraries for doing this. In fact, the hmac library which ships with Python is built for just this purpose.

Let's say that Alice wants to send a message to Bob. And let's also say that Alice and Bob agree to share a secret password p@55w0rd with each other before the messages are sent.

Alice creates a message and concatenates it with p@55w0rd; then she computes a hash of the message:

```
from hashlib import sha256

message = "Hello Bob, Let's meet at the Kruger National Park on
2020-12-12 at 1pm."
hash_message = sha256(("p@55w0rd" + message).encode()).
hexdigest()
```

The computed hash is 39aae6ffdb3c0ac1c1cc0f50bf08871a729052 cf1133c4c9b44a5bab8fb66211. Alice then sends this message, including the hash to Bob, who will now verify that only Alice could've sent it:

```
from hashlib import sha256

alices_message = "Hello Bob, Let's meet at the Kruger National
Park on 2020-12-12 at 1pm."
```

```
alices_hash = "39aae6ffdb3c0ac1c1cc0f50bf08871a729052cf1133c4c
9b44a5bab8fb66211"
hash_message = sha256(("p@55w0rd" + alices_message).encode()).
hexdigest()

if hash_message == alices_hash:
    print("Message has not been tampered with")
```

This is a trivial example of a digital signature to give you a taste of how they work. We'll soon see that the libraries responsible for verifying and signing the messages are more robust and don't require the use of a pre-shared key.

Symmetric cryptography

Symmetric cryptography is the oldest form of cryptography. It involves *sharing* a key (cipher) with the person you want to communicate with.

For example, let's say you want to share your car with your brother. You make a copy of the key and give the key to him. Now, only you and your brother are able start the car. But while you're on holiday, your brother calls to tell you that the key has been lost, and somebody may have stolen it.

This example illustrates some of the problems with symmetric cryptography—the primary problem being your placement of trust in the counter-party, and the overhead and maintenance of the list of authorized people who may drive your car. Also, you may not know when a particular key has been compromised. Let's look at a classic example of symmetric cryptography.

Caesar's Cipher

In Rome, circa 50 BC, Julius Caesar used a method of encryption for his personal correspondence. It's a simple method of symmetric encryption that works by shifting the characters in a message by a fixed amount.

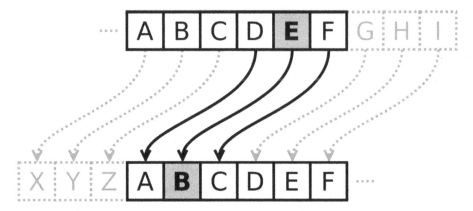

Figure 6-1. *A Caesar Cipher*

Ahead of time, Caesar would give the recipient the cipher (key) of say 3. And a D would become an A in the encrypted message. The recipient would apply the reverse and an A would become a D.

The problem here is that the act of sending the cipher is insecure—any form of communication can be spied on and the key ascertained. We need a form of encryption free from the act of creating and sending shared keys. This is why public key cryptography was invented and solves the problem of shared trust.

Public key cryptography

Public key cryptography is an example of *asymmetric* cryptography. It's the type of cryptography that secures almost all modern systems on the Internet. We're going to look at it from a simple level so that you get a gist of how and why it works, and then we'll get more technical and granular with some examples mixed in.

Public key cryptography involves not one but two (or more) key pairs, one of which is kept secret. There are many different public key cryptography algorithms, but we'll be using the popular RSA (Rivest, Shamir, Adleman—the creators) algorithm (in the case of Bitcoin, the

ECDSA (Elliptic Curve Digital Signature Algorithm) is used instead). These algorithms are complicated mathematical gems beyond the scope of this book, and they ship in a variety of flavors prized for certain properties: some are thought to be quantum computing-resistant; others are chosen for their speed or ease. But the output of any of these algorithms is the same: a *correlated* pair of keys, A and B, that you can use for the purposes of encrypting a message to be sent over an insecure channel.

Note the word *correlated*—the keys A and B are linked in a mathematical way. A must be kept secret, known only to you. But B is your *public* key—you can publicize it on the Internet, and someone can use it to encrypt a message that *only you* can decrypt (using A). You can effectively send your B to anyone wishing to communicate with you in a secure manner, but you should guard A like Frodo did the Ring. We use public key cryptography all the time—mostly without realizing it—when you access a website over https, you're using the website's B to encrypt your outgoing data so that only the website may read it.

Additionally—and this is really important—you can use your private key A to *sign* a message, and B (known to the public) can *verify* the signature. This is how transactions on a blockchain are validated. But more on that later. Let's first look at some examples to get this sticking.

An Example in Python

Here's a fantastic analogy from the excellent open source Python NaCL library:

> Imagine Alice wants something valuable shipped to her.
> Because it's valuable, she wants to make sure it arrives
> securely (i.e., hasn't been opened or tampered with) and
> that it's not a forgery (i.e., it's actually from the sender
> she's expecting it to be from and nobody's pulling the old
> switcheroo).

One way she can do this is by providing the sender (let's call him Bob) with a high- security box of her choosing. She provides Bob with this box, and something else: a padlock, but a padlock without a key. Alice is keeping that key all to herself. Bob can put items in the box then put the padlock onto it. But once the padlock snaps shut, the box cannot be opened by anyone who doesn't have Alice's private key.

Here's the twist though: Bob also puts a padlock onto the box. This padlock uses a key Bob has published to the world, such that if you have one of Bob's keys, you know a box came from him because Bob's keys will open Bob's padlocks (let's imagine a world where padlocks cannot be forged even if you know the key). Bob then sends the box to Alice.

In order for Alice to open the box, she needs two keys: her private key that opens her own padlock and Bob's well-known key. If Bob's key doesn't open the second padlock, then Alice knows that this is not the box she was expecting from Bob, it's a forgery.

This bidirectional guarantee around identity is known as mutual authentication.

We're going to be using PyNaCl to walk through an example of the preceding analogy in Python. First things first, let's install PyNaCl:

Note   By the way, PyNaCl is a great example of a well-tested library to use in your own projects. Most importantly—for a cryptographic library—it has great documentation littered with examples. You can read more about it here: `https://pynacl.readthedocs.io/en/stable/public/`

```
poetry add pynacl
```

Then let's activate our virtual environment and spawn a Python interpreter:

```
poetry shell
ipython
```

We're going to use the given analogy to drive the concepts home. Bob and Alice will both generate their own public-private key pairs, and Bob will encrypt a message to Alice, for her to decrypt. PyNaCl supplies us with a very useful Box class which mimics the preceding analogy.

Let's go:

```
from nacl.public import PrivateKey, Box

# Generate secret keys for Alice and Bob
alices_private_key = PrivateKey.generate()
bobs_private_key = PrivateKey.generate()

# Public keys are generated from the private keys
alices_public_key = alices_private_key.public_key
bobs_public_key = bobs_private_key.public_key

# Bob will send Alice a message...
# So he makes a Box with his private key and Alice's public key
bobs_box = Box(bobs_private_key, alices_public_key)

# We encrypt Bob's secret message (bytes)...
encrypted = bobs_box.encrypt(b"I am Satoshi")

# Alice creates a second box with her private key and Bob's
# public key so that she can decrypt the message
alices_box = Box(alices_private_key, bobs_public_key)

# Now Alice can decrypt the message:
plaintext = alices_box.decrypt(encrypted)
print(plaintext.decode('utf-8'))

I am Satoshi
```

PyNaCl will raise an exception if the message was tampered with or couldn't be decrypted.

Digital signatures

Digital signatures exist for many of the same reasons you may sign something in real life: they leave the recipient no room to doubt the authenticity of the document. They satisfy three useful claims:

1. Authenticity: "This could've only been signed by Daniel."

2. Integrity: "This data wasn't forged or tampered with."

3. Non-repudiation: "Daniel can't deny having sent the data."

Digital signatures make use of public key cryptography to satisfy these claims. Much like in our example, where Alice creates a "box" with Bob's public key, we use Bob's public key to verify that only Bob could've sent and signed a piece of data. The idea is simple: anyone with my public key can quickly verify that I did indeed sign a message.

Here's a diagram of the given idea.

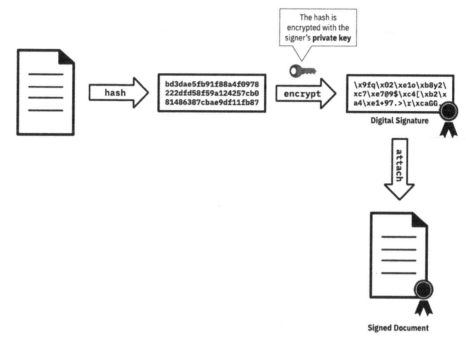

Figure 6-2. *Digitally signing a document*

1. First, our unencrypted, plaintext data is hashed (prevents tampering).

2. Then the hash is encrypted using the private key.

3. Then we attach (concatenate) the encrypted hash to the data.

Let's see what this looks like in Python. First, from Bob's perspective, we'll create a key pair; then sign a message with it. After, we'll see how anyone can use that public key to verify the message.

```
1  import nacl.encoding
2  import nacl.signing
3
4  # Generate a new key-pair for Bob
```

```
 5  bobs_private_key = nacl.signing.SigningKey.generate()
 6  bobs_public_key = bobs_private_key.verify_key
 7
 8  # Since it's bytes, we'll need to serialize the key to a
       readable format before publishing it:
 9  bobs_public_key_hex = bobs_public_key.encode(encoder=nacl.
    encoding.HexEncoder)
10
11  # Now, let's sign a message with it
12  signed = bobs_private_key.sign(b"Send $37 to Alice")
```

The public key (in hex) generated on line 10 was

e7ff10ede8a691b982516059a0627d369504e3633e0297e28ec5fc71994577d3

Firstly, let's see what the signed message looks like on line 12. As you can see, the message is not encrypted! But it is padded with bytes containing the signature:

```
b'\x9fq\x02\xe1o\xb8y2\xc7\xe7@9$\xc4[\xb2\xa4\xe1+97.>\r\
xcaGG\x8a
Y\x86\xc3\xfe\xb9W{\xc4\x9c\x87\x00(\x1d\xe9}j\xe4\xed\xd2\x0b\
xcb\x88\x87J\xecy\x04GQ
H\xea\xcc\xc2\xe7\x03Send $37 to Alice'
```

Verification

The verification process uses the signer's public key to check the signature.

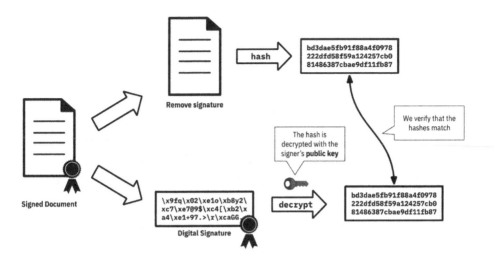

Figure 6-3. *Verifying a digital signature*

Let's see how we can use the public key to verify that the message was signed by Bob:

```
1   import nacl.encoding
2   import nacl.signing
3
4
5   # From the above example...
6   bobs_public_key = b'e7ff10ede8a691b982516059a0627d369504e36
    33e0297e28ec5fc71994577d3'
7
8   # We generate the verify_key
9   verify_key = nacl.signing.VerifyKey(bobs_public_key,
    encoder=nacl.encoding.HexEncoder)
10
11  signed_message = b'\x9fq\x02\xe1o\xb8y2\xc7\xe7@9$\xc4[\
    xb2\xa4\xe1+97.>\r\xca GG\x8a Y\x86\xc3\xfe\xb9W{\xc4\x9c\
    x87\x00(\x1d\xe9}j\xe4\xed\xd2\x0b\xcb\x88\x87 J\xecy\
    x04GQH\xea\xcc\xc2\xe7\x03Send $37 to Alice'
```

```
12
13   # Now we attempt to verify the message
14   # Any invalidation will result in an Exception being thrown
15   verify_key.verify(signed_message)
```

> **Note**   Does the preceding example make sense? It's good to take a pause and play around in the Python interpreter until you get the gist of using NaCl. It's going to become important as we go through the next chapter on transactions.

Wallets on the Blockchain

Unlike Bitcoin, Ethereum is an account-based model—meaning each "user" on the Blockchain would have an account. Bitcoin doesn't have the notion of an *account*; instead, it's a system that closely resembles the way cash flows in and out of a physical wallet. The Bitcoin system is called UTXO (Unspent Transaction Outputs), and it's an elegant data structure for modeling transactions. We'll talk about UTXOs in the next chapter, but for now let's focus on the account-based model of Ethereum.

When you initially interact with Ethereum, the first thing you usually do is generate a key pair. Your Ethereum *address* is just your public key. Your private key is stored somewhere safe, either in some sort of software or on a hardware wallet. For someone to send you money over the Ethereum blockchain, they just need to know your public key. But only you can access that money because only you hold the private key.

CHAPTER 7

Creating a Transactional Node

To attain a fully fledged cryptocurrency, the data in our blockchain must be *transactions*. Each transaction transfers ownership of coins from one private key to another. The transactions are collected in each block and *mined*, growing the blockchain; in fact, the older a block is, the more surety it has—it's more likely to be part of the de facto blockchain. At any given time, miners are busy mining slightly different blocks containing different transactions—it's a race to find a block—when a miner finds a block, they broadcast it, and the rest of the miners drop their current blocks (they've lost the race) and move on to the next one. These "dropped" blocks are usually called orphaned blocks.

In this chapter, we'll wrangle all the concepts we've learned and incorporate them into a full node capable of operating in a peer-to-peer network. Then, using the previous chapter's cryptography, we'll clarify how transactions are made and verified.

© Daniel van Flymen 2020
D. van Flymen, *Learn Blockchain by Building One*,
https://doi.org/10.1007/978-1-4842-5171-3_7

Transactions and Work Summary

A departure from Bitcoin's UTXO Model

If you've spent any time investigating Bitcoin, then you're likely to have heard of UTXOs or, more formally, Unspent Transaction Outputs (UTXOs). This model is elegant because it resembles the way that cold, hard cash works in the real world-there are no accounts: money is a "note" that may reside in someone's wallet (public key). UTXOs are contrasted to an account-based model, which is roughly how your bank account works: you give someone your account number, and they may transfer money to it. Some cryptocurrencies use this model, most notably Ethereum.

This is the model we'll be implementing, because it's easy to reason about, test, and explain. We'll be designing the class in such a way that it may be easily swapped out for a UTXO model (left as an exercise to the reader).

The role of a miner

As we saw in Chapter 4, the role of a miner is to generate new coins by finding an appropriate hash for a block. While mining, a miner collects incoming transaction in a pool—known as the mempool in Bitcoin—waiting to be included in the subsequent block. If there are too many transactions to fill a block, then a miner picks the ones with the highest fees to increase profits. During the 2017 cryptocurrency boom, the price of Bitcoin transactions exceeded $40 because of how many transactions were backed up. Topics of scaling Bitcoin often include the mempool and transaction fees, most notably the question of block size: how many transactions should we store in a block? In Bitcoin the limit is 1 megabyte worth, which is on average around 1700 transactions.

How we'll be implementing transactions

We'll be making some changes to our funcoin node; specifically, we must figure out how transactions propagate across our network. The way that p2p networks are structured is crucial to the reliability of a cryptocurrency. Bitcoin is considered a "push" network: instead of a node querying its peers for new transactions, a node *pushes* a new transaction to all its peers when it receives one. Loosely speaking, when a new node joins a network, it should create a *gossip* effect whereby peers of peers learn about its presence and can reliably send it future transactions.

A transaction has a simple data structure, containing

1.   Sender's public key

2.   Recipient's public key

3.   Amount to be transferred

4.   An advertised fee (think "tip," to incentivize miners to include the transaction in their next block)

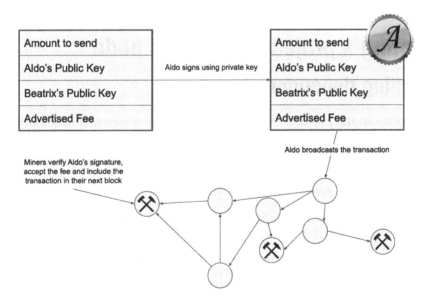

Figure 7-1. Creating a transaction using digital signatures

In order to send or receive funcoins, we need to generate a wallet—a public-private key pair. To send funcoins to Beatrix, Aldo must create a transaction containing both his and Beatrix's **public** keys and the amount to be sent. The transaction is then signed using Aldo's **private** key.

Any peers in the network can validate the transaction as authentic by inspecting Aldo's public key. If the transaction passes validation, then it will later be added to the blockchain when a miner includes it.

Errata and Changes

As dependencies and libraries change, and people discover bugs in this initial implementation, over time it will become inevitable that the working code will diverge from the print, hopefully in a minor way. Please keep the public GitHub repository handy should you need to tug on a helpful thread: `https://github.com/dvf/learn-blockchains-book/`.

Creating a project for our full node

Installing dependencies

At this point in the project, we've covered all the atomic units necessary to construct our node:

- A blockchain for maintaining an immutable chain of data

- A server for allowing clients to connect and send data back and forth

- A mining algorithm for creating new funcoins

- Cryptography basics to allow us to verify and construct transactions

We now need to consider the architecture of our node and restructure our project, using the given atomic units as importable modules. We'll create a fresh Python project (folder) to do this. Let's create a new folder and initiate it as a blank Poetry project:

```
$ mkdir funcoin
$ cd funcoin
$ poetry init -n
```

And add the necessary dependencies (I'll discuss what each is for in a minute):

```
$ poetry add pynacl structlog colorama marshmallow marshmallow-oneofschema aiohttp
```

Note   You may notice the addition of *structlog*—later, we'll use it in place of the `print()`statements we have littered throughout our code to give us slick, meaningful output.

Poetry will now create a virtualenv in an appropriate place, and install the dependencies:

```
Creating virtualenv funcoin-PPSjSr3P-py3.8 in
/Users/dvf/Library/Caches/pypoetry/virtualenvs
Using version ^20.1.0 for structlog
Using version ^1.3.0 for pynacl
```

```
Updating dependencies
Resolving dependencies... (1.2s)

Writing lock file

Package operations: 22 installs, 0 updates, 0 removals

  - Installing idna (2.9)
  - Installing multidict (4.7.6)
  - Installing pycparser (2.20)
  - Installing pyparsing (2.4.7)
  - Installing six (1.14.0)
  - Installing async-timeout (3.0.1)
  - Installing attrs (19.3.0)
  - Installing cffi (1.14.0)
  - Installing chardet (3.0.4)
  - Installing colorama (0.4.3)
  - Installing marshmallow (3.6.0)
  - Installing  more-itertools  (8.3.0)
  - Installing packaging (20.3)
  - Installing pluggy (0.13.1)
  - Installing py (1.8.1)
  - Installing wcwidth (0.1.9)
  - Installing yarl (1.4.2)
  - Installing aiohttp (3.6.2)
  - Installing marshmallow-oneofschema (2.0.1)
  - Installing pynacl (1.3.0)
  - Installing pytest (5.4.2)
  - Installing structlog (20.1.0)
```

You should now have a `pyproject.toml` and `poetry.lock` files in your funcoin project. Here's a summary of what we'll be using each package for:

Package	Description
Pynacl	Signing and validating transactions
Structlog	Logging library (better than `print()` statements)
Colorama	Allows colorful output (in logging)
Marshmallow	Validates data structures, such as JSON messages that our node will send and receive
marshmallow-oneofschema	Allows marshmallow to validate more complex data structures
Aiohttp	An asynchronous HTTP client (we'll need this to find our public IP address)

Creating the file structure

We're now going to create a nested funcoin folder to house our "atomic" units—the different aspects or classes that when combined give us a full node. Create empty files for the following:

```
touch node.py
mkdir funcoin
cd funcoin
touch __init__.py
touch blockchain.py
touch connections.py
touch transactions.py
touch server.py
```

```
touch types.py
touch messages.py
touch utils.py
```

Your complete folder should look like this:

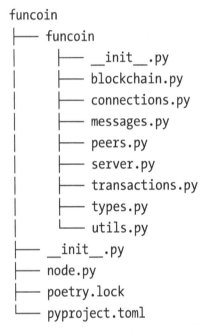

```
funcoin
├── funcoin
│      ├── __init__.py
│      ├── blockchain.py
│      ├── connections.py
│      ├── messages.py
│      ├── peers.py
│      ├── server.py
│      ├── transactions.py
│      ├── types.py
│      └── utils.py
├── __init__.py
├── node.py
├── poetry.lock
└── pyproject.toml
```

The empty files inside funcoin/funcoin will contain our soon-to-be restructured code from the previous chapters. Let's examine the structure for our node.

Structuring our node

Delegating responsibilities

We're going to use node.py as the entrypoint for running our node. "What's an entrypoint?" you ask. Think of it as the canonical way to run our node. I find it helpful, when designing programs, to be as abstract as possible— design how you want the program to run before implementing anything:

```
# Instantiate the server with some config
server = Server(**some_config)

# Start the server
server.run()
```

Pause here for a brief moment and think about the various parts that we'll be implementing: do you think our fake Server() class should be responsible for holding our blockchain? How about making transactions? If it's responsible for running *everything*, then how will be swap out our transactions model for, say, UTXOs at a later point?

A sound principle when designing applications is that *each module should be responsible for doing one thing and doing it well*. Here's a better way of abstracting our server:

```
from funcoin.blockchain import Blockchain
from funcoin.pool import ConnectionPool
from funcoin.server import Server

# Instantiate  the  blockchain  and our pool for "peers"
blockchain = Blockchain()
connection_pool = ConnectionPool()

# Instantiate the server and "bolt on" our modules
server = Server(blockchain, connection_pool)

# Now start the server
server.start()
```

Now, we have a much cleaner abstraction—our server need not concern itself with the blockchain at all; it just needs to worry about being a server. Without explaining the various modules right now, here's what our final node.py looks like.

Listing 7-1. funcoin/node.py

```
1   import asyncio
2
3   from funcoin.blockchain import Blockchain
4   from funcoin.connections import ConnectionPool
5   from funcoin.peers import P2PProtocol
6   from funcoin.server import Server
7
8   blockchain = Blockchain() ①
9   connection_pool = ConnectionPool() ②
10
11  server = Server(blockchain, connection_pool, P2PProtocol)
12
13
14  async def main():
15      # Start the server
16      await server.listen()
17
18
19  asyncio.run(main())
```

Notice the instantiation of the Connectionpool ① and Blockchain classes ②. This ensures that they re stateful singletons—meaning that any module doing a from node import connection_pool will be importing the same instantiated object, thus maintaining state.

Let's set the goal of our four critical modules before implementing them.

Module	Description
blockchain	Module to house our Blockchain class containing the de facto blockchain we built in earlier chapters
Peers	Logic to handle the propagation of messages that peers may send us: how we communicate. We'll call this the P2PProtocol
connections	Logic to handle the "pool" of active connections communicating with our node
server	Where our basic TCP Server lives

Note   Since we're using asyncio (as opposed to threads), we're vastly simplifying the concurrency problem: when using threads the programmer needs to worry about race conditions (two or more threads compete to update or receive something).The downside of this approach is that the code can become difficult to read and reason about (but in my experience, well worth it if you take the time to follow it).

Our entrypoint has a single function main(). Typical of an asyncio program, it's used to spin up our server.

The server module

We'll be transforming the chat server we created in Chapter 5 and adapting it for our purpose, in funcoin/server.py.

Here's the rough outline for our class.

Listing 7-2. server.py

```
class Server:
    def __init__ (self, blockchain, connection_pool, p2p_
    protocol):
        ...

    async def get_external_ip(self):
        # Finds our "external IP" so that we can advertize it
          to our peers
        ...

    async def handle_connection(self, reader: StreamReader,
    writer: StreamWriter):
        # This function is called when we receive a new
          connection
        # The `writer` object represents the connecting peer

        while True:
            try:
                # We handle and/or reply to the incoming data
                ...

            except (asyncio.exceptions.IncompleteReadError,
            ConnectionError):
                # An error happened, break out of the wait loop
                break
    async def listen(self, hostname="0.0.0.0", port=8888):
        # This is the listen method which spawns our server

        server = await asyncio.start_server(self.handle_
        connection, hostname, port)
```

```
        logger.info(f"Server listening on {hostname}:{port}")

        async with server:
            await server.serve_forever()
```

Let's flesh out the methods, sequentially. Do not be alarmed if you don't "get it" upon first inspection; we'll be revisiting the server frequently as we keep bootstrapping our modules.

Listing 7-3. funcoin/node.py

```
1   import asyncio
2   from asyncio import StreamReader, StreamWriter
3
4   import structlog
5   from marshmallow.exceptions import MarshmallowError
6
7   from funcoin.messages import BaseSchema
8   from funcoin.utils import get_external_ip
9
10  logger = structlog.getLogger() ⑦
11
12
13  class Server:
14      def __init__(self, blockchain, connection_pool,
        p2p_protocol):
15          self.blockchain = blockchain ①
16          self.connection_pool = connection_pool
17          self.p2p_protocol = p2p_protocol
18          self.external_ip = None
19          self.external_port = None
20
21          if not (blockchain and 22 connection_pool and
            p2p_protocol):
```

```
22              logger.error("'blockchain', 'connection_pool', and
                'gossip_protocol' must all be instantiated")
23              raise Exception("Could not start")
24
25      async def get_external_ip(self):
26          self.external_ip = await get_external_ip() ②
27
28      async def handle_connection(self, reader: StreamReader,
        writer: StreamWriter):
29          while True:
30              try:
31                  # Wait forever on new data to arrive
32                  data = await reader.readuntil(b"\n") ③
33
34                  decoded_data = data.decode("utf8").strip() ④
35
36                  try:
37                      message = BaseSchema().loads(decoded_
                        data) ⑤
38                  except  MarshmallowError:
39                      logger.info("Received unreadable
                        message", peer=writer)
40                      break
41
42                  # Extract the address from the message, add
                      it to the writer object
43                  writer.address = message["meta"]["address"]
44
45                  # Let's add the peer to our connection pool
46                  self.connection_pool.add_peer(writer)
47
```

```
48                    #...and handle the message
49                    await self.p2p_protocol.handle_
                      message(message, writer) ⑥
50
51                    await writer.drain()
52                    if writer.is_closing():
53                        break
54
55             except (asyncio.exceptions.IncompleteReadError,
               ConnectionError):
56                 # An error happened, break out of the wait loop
57                 break
58
59         # The connection has closed. Let's clean up...
60         writer.close()
61         await  writer.wait_closed()
62         self.connection_pool.remove_peer(writer)⑦
63
64     async def listen(self, hostname="0.0.0.0", port=8888):
65         server = await asyncio.start_server(self.handle_
               connection, hostname, port)
66         logger.info(f"Server listening on {hostname}:{port}")
67
68         self.external_ip = await self.get_external_ip()
69         self.external_port = 8888
70
71         async with server:
72             await server.serve_forever()
```

① This is how we "bootstrap" our modules to the server: the server class (and anything attached to it) will always have access to our blockchain via self.blockchain.

② Although we haven't implemented get_external_ip() yet, it's responsible for finding our external IP address.

③ Here, we wait *forever* until a message is sent to us terminated by a new line (\n) character. This is the first of some potential vulnerabilities that you should be on the lookout for, since anyone could just spam our server with a never-ending message.

④ We try to decode the message by assuming it was sent to us as a UTF-8-formatted string.

⑤ Perhaps the biggest surprise we'll learn about shortly is the usage of marshmallow (the library we installed earlier) to parse and validate an incoming message from a peer.

⑥ Once the message has been parsed successfully, further code can assume that all relevant fields exist, and we can use our p2p protocol to figure out what to do.

⑦ Notice the import and usage of *structlog*—we're using it to replace the print() statements. It gives highly readable output to the console when we run our entire node. For example, it tells you which file the log came from.

It's not important that you grasp the minutiae of details of what we've implemented in the Server class. Rather, zoom out and follow the overall logic, taking into account the bigger principles at play.

The blockchain module

Let's revisit the Blockchain class we built in Chapter 3 and paste it in funcoin/blockchain.py.

Listing 7-4. funcoin/blockchain.py

```
1   import asyncio
2   import json
3   import math
4   import random
5   from hashlib import sha256
6   from time import time
7
8   import structlog
9
10  logger = structlog.getLogger("blockchain")
11
12
13  class Blockchain(object):
14      def __init__ (self):
15          self.chain = []
16          self.pending_transactions = []
17          self.target = "0000ffffffffffffffffffffffffffffffffff
            ffffffffffffffffffffffffffff"
18
19          # Create the genesis block
20          logger.info("Creating genesis block")
```

```
21              self.chain.append(self.new_block())
22
23      def new_block(self):
24          block = self.create_block(
25              height=len(self.chain),
26              transactions=self.pending_transactions,
27              previous_hash=self.last_block["hash"] if
                 self.last_block else None,
28              nonce=format(random.getrandbits(64), "x"),
29              target=self.target,
30              timestamp=time(),
31          )
32
33          # Reset the list of pending transactions
34          self.pending_transactions = []
35
36          return block
37
38      @staticmethod
39  def create_block(
40      height, transactions, previous_hash, nonce,
        target, timestamp=None
41  ):
42          block = {
43              "height": height,
44              "transactions": transactions,
45              "previous_hash": previous_hash,
46              "nonce": nonce,
47              "target": target,
48              "timestamp": timestamp or time(),
49          }
50
```

```
51        # Get the hash of this new block, and add it to
              the block
52        block_string = json.dumps(block, sort_keys=True).
          encode()
53        block["hash"] = sha256(block_string).hexdigest()
54        return block
55
56    @staticmethod
57    def hash(block):
58        # We ensure the dictionary is sorted or we'll have
              inconsistent hashes
59        block_string = json.dumps(block, sort_keys=True).
          encode()
60        return sha256(block_string).hexdigest()
61
62    @property
63    def last_block(self):
64        # Returns the last block in the chain (if there
              are blocks)
65        return self.chain[-1] if self.chain else None
66
67    def valid_block(self, block):
68        # Check if a block's hash is less than the
              target...
69        return block["hash"] < self.target
70
71    def add_block(self,  block):
72        # TODO: Add proper validation logic here!
73        self.chain.append(block)
74
```

```
75      def recalculate_target(self, block_index):
76          """
77          Returns the number we need to get below to mine a
            block
78          """
79          # Check if we need to recalculate the target
80          if block_index % 10 == 0:
81              # Expected time span of 10 blocks
82              expected_timespan = 10 * 10
83
84              # Calculate the actual time span
85              actual_timespan = self.chain[-1]["timestamp"] -
                self.chain[-10]["timestamp"]
86
87              # Figure out what the offset is
88              ratio = actual_timespan / expected_timespan
89
90              # Now let's adjust the ratio to not be too
                extreme
91              ratio = max(0.25, ratio)
92              ratio = min(4.00, ratio)
93
94              # Calculate the new target by multiplying the
                current one by the ratio
95              new_target = int(self.target, 16) * ratio
96
97              self.target = format(math.floor(new_target),
                "x").zfill(64)
98              logger.info(f"Calculated new mining target:
                {self.target}")
99
100         return self.target
```

```
101
102        async def get_blocks_after_timestamp(self, timestamp):
103            for index, block in enumerate(self.chain):
104                if timestamp < block["timestamp"]:
105                    return self.chain[index:]
106
107        async def mine_new_block(self):
108            self.recalculate_target(self.last_block["index"] + 1)
109            while True:
110                new_block = self.new_block()
111                if self.valid_block(new_block):
112                    break
113
114                await asyncio.sleep(0)
115
116            self.chain.append(new_block)
117            logger.info("Found a new block: ", new_block)
```

The only change here is the addition of structlog, where we've replaced each print() statement with a helpful logger instead.

The connections module

In funcoin/connections.py we're going to store all the logic that manages our ConnectionPool from our chat server in Chapter 5. Here's the outline of the class:

```
class ConnectionPool:
    def __init__ (self):
        ...

    def broadcast(self, message):
```

```
        # Method to broadcast a message to all connected peers
        ...

    @staticmethod
    def get_address_string(writer):
        # Get a peer's ip:port (address)
        ...

    def add_peer(self, writer):
        # Add a peer to our connection pool
        ...

    def remove_peer(self, writer):
        # Remove a peer from our connection pool
        ...

    def get_alive_peers(self, count):
        # Return some connected peers
        ...
```

Let's see what the fleshed-out implementation looks like. Since most of these methods were already fleshed out in Chapter 5, there should be no surprises here. The main change is the additional methods: get_alive_peers() and get_address_string().

Listing 7-5. funcoin/blockchain.py

```
1  import structlog
2  from more_itertools import take
3
4  logger = structlog.getLogger(__name__)
5
6
7  class ConnectionPool:
8      def __init__ (self):
```

```
9            self.connection_pool = dict() ①
10
11       def broadcast(self,  message):
12           for user in self.connection_pool:
13               user.write(f"{message}".encode())
14
15       @staticmethod
16       def get_address_string(writer):
17           ip = writer.address["ip"]
18           port = writer.address["port"]
19           return f"{ip}:{port}" ②
20
21       def add_peer(self, writer):
22           address = self.get_address_string(writer)
23           self.connection_pool[address] = writer
24           logger.info("Added new peer to pool",
                 address=address)
25
26       def remove_peer(self, writer):
27           address = self.get_address_string(writer)
28           self.connection_pool.pop(address)
29           logger.info("Removed peer from pool",
                 address=address)
30
31       def get_alive_peers(self, count):
32           # TODO (Reader): Sort these by most active, but
                 let's just get the first *count* of them for now
33           return take(count, self.connection_pool.items()) ③
```

① Here we use a `dict`, mapping `address` to `writer` (representing the peer connection).

② The `address` string in the mapping is simply the `ip:port` combination of the peer—this is important because it's how we'll uniquely identify connections.

③ We use the `take()` function to return `count` number of peers from our pool.

The peers module

This is perhaps the most important module thus far: it represents the logic surrounding the sending and receiving of messages in our P2P network. Let's stub out the methods in `funcoin/peers.py`; they're going to be surprisingly simple:

```python
class P2PError(Exception): ①
    pass

class P2PProtocol:
    def __init__ (self, server):
        ...

    @staticmethod
    async def send_message(writer, message):
        # Sends a message to a particular peer (the writer
          object)
        ...

    async def handle_message(self, message, writer):
        # Handles an incoming message passed by the server
        # Hands this message off to a more specific method:
          handle_<method name>()
```

```
    ...

async def handle_ping(self, message, writer):
    # Handles in incoming "ping" message
    ...

async def handle_block(self, message, writer):
    # Handles in incoming "block" message
    ...

async def handle_transaction(self, message, writer):
    # Handles in incoming "transaction" message
    ...

async def handle_peers(self, message, writer):
    # Handles in incoming "peers" message
    ...
```

① We'll need an error class that we can use to "catch"
for problems from the importing code.

The comments in each method explain the code that we need to
implement. The most important method here is the handle_message()
method. We haven't yet defined the messages that each peer can send, so
let's define the basic form of a message:

```
{
    "meta": {
        "address": {
            "ip": <external ip: str>,
            "port": <external port: int>
        },
        "client": "funcoin 0.1"
    },
```

```
  "message": {
    "name": <message name: str>,
    "payload": <message payload: object>
  }
}
```

That is, *all* messages sent in our p2p network share this structure. The meta key contains information about the peer sending the message (even if that peer is us), while the message key contains the name and payload of the message being sent. For funcoin we'll be implementing four messages.

Message Name	Description
Ping	The initial message that a node sends to a peer when initiating a connection
Transaction	A single transaction that propagates throughout from peer to peer
Peers	A bunch of addresses that a peer may or may not know about (to build their network)
Block	A single block (perhaps recently mined) for a peer to add to their blockchain

Before we talk in depth about what these messages look like, let's complete the funcoin/peers.py module by fleshing out the given methods.

Listing 7-6. funcoin/peers.py

```
1  import asyncio
2
3  import structlog
4  from funcoin.messages import (
5      create_peers_message,
6      create_block_message,
```

```
 7    create_transaction_message,
 8    create_ping_message,
 9  )
10  from funcoin.transactions import validate_transaction
11
12  logger = structlog.getLogger(__name__)
13
14
15  class P2PError(Exception):
16      pass
17
18
19  class P2PProtocol:
20      def __init__ (self, server):
21          self.server = server
22          self.blockchain = server.blockchain
23          self.connection_pool = server.connection_pool
24
25      @staticmethod
26      async def send_message(writer, message):
27          writer.write(message.encode() + b"\n")
28
29      async def handle_message(self, message, writer):
30          message_handlers = {
31              "block": self.handle_block,
32              "ping": self.handle_ping,
33              "peers": self.handle_peers,
34              "transaction": self.handle_transaction,
35          }
36
37          handler = message_handlers.get(message["name"])
```

```
38          if not handler:
39              raise P2PError("Missing handler for message")
40
41          await handler(message, writer)
42
43      async def handle_ping(self, message, writer):
44          block_height = message["payload"]["block_height"]
45
46          # If they're a miner, let's mark them as such
47          writer.is_miner = message["payload"]["is_miner"]
48
49          # Let's send our 20 most "alive" peers to this user
50          peers = self.connection_pool.get_alive_peers(20)
51          peers_message = create_peers_message(self.server.
            external_ip, self.server.external_port, peers
52          await self.send_message(writer, peers_message)
53
54          # Let's send them blocks if they have less than us
55          if block_height < self.blockchain.last_block
            ["height"]:
56              # Send them each block in succession, from
                  their height
57              for block in self.blockchain.chain
                [block_height + 1:]:
51                  await self.send_message(
52                      writer,
53                      create_block_message(
54                          self.server.external_ip, self.
                            server.external_port, block
55                      ),
56                  )
57
```

```
58      async def handle_transaction(self, message, writer):
59          """
60          Executed when we receive a transaction that was
            broadcast by a peer
61          """
62          logger.info("Received transaction")
63
64          # Validate the transaction
65          tx = message["payload"]
66
67          if validate_transaction(tx) is True:
68              # Add the tx to our pool, and propagate it to
                  our peers
69              if tx not in self.blockchain.pending_transactions:
70                  self.blockchain.pending_transactions.append(tx)
71
72                  for peer in self.connection_pool.get_alive_
                    peers(20):
73                      await self.send_message(
74                          peer,
75                          create_transaction_message(
76                              self.server.external_ip, self.
                                server.external_port, tx
77                          ),
78                      )
79          else:
80              logger.warning("Received invalid transaction")
81
82      async def handle_block(self, message, writer):
83          """
84          Executed when we receive a block that was broadcast
            by a peer
85          """
```

```
86          logger.info("Received new block")
87
88          block = message["payload"]
89
90          # Give the block to the blockain to append if valid
91          self.blockchain.add_block(block)
92
93          # Transmit the block to our peers
94          for peer in self.connection_pool.get_alive_peers(20):
95              await self.send_message(
96                  peer,
97                  create_block_message(
98                      self.server.external_ip, self.server.
                          external_port, block
99                  ),
100             )
101
102     async def handle_peers(self, message, writer):
103         """
104         Executed when we receive a block that was broadcast
            by a peer
105         """
106         logger.info("Received new peers")
107
108         peers = message["payload"]
109
110         # Craft a ping message for us to send to each peer
111         ping_message = create_ping_message(
112             self.server.external_ip,
113             self.server.external_port,
114             len(self.blockchain.chain),
```

```
115              len(self.connection_pool.get_alive_peers(50)),
116              False,
117          )
118
119      for peer in peers:
120              # Create a connection and add them to our
                   connection pool if successful
121              reader, writer = await asyncio.open_connection
                 (peer["ip"], peer["port"])
122
123              # We're only interested in the "writer"
124              self.connection_pool.add_peer(writer)
125
126              # Send the peer a PING message
127              await self.send_message(writer, ping_message)
```

Take special note of the handle_ping method (I've added comments to aid with the explanation). But at this point, it's worthwhile discussing the structure of the messages sent in our cryptocurrency.

Messaging

Previously, we showed a JSON example of the generic form of a message; here's what it looks like as a table:

Table 7-1. *Generic Message form*

Field name	Type	Description
Meta	meta	—
Message	message	—

The meta object is included in every message and contains information pertaining to the sender.

Table 7-2. *meta object*

Field name	Type	Description
address	Peer	Contains the network address information of the node who sent this message
client	String	The name (of version) of the client who sent the message. For example, funcoin-0.1

The peer type is fairly generic too. It appears in lists of peers being sent, for example, a new node joining a network, or in the meta block of every message sent.

Table 7-3. *peer type (represents a peer)*

Field name	Type	Description
Ip	string	The public IP of the peer
Port	Int	The port the peer is listening on
last_seen	Int	UTC timestamp of the last seen time of the peer

Now, let's look at the structures of the four types of messages in our network. The message key is simple; each message has a name and a payload (changes depending on the type of message sent):

Table 7-4. *message object*

Field name	Type	Description
Name	string	The name of the message (so that the receiver knows how to parse it)
Payload	object	The message payload corresponding to the message type. See the next section for the different payloads

Let's define the different kinds of payloads.

Table 7-5. ping payload

Key	Value			
Name	Pong			
Payload	**Key**		**Type**	**Example**
	block_height		int	2000
	peer_count		int	23
	is_miner		bool	False .

Table 7-6. transaction payload

Key	Value		
Name	Transaction		
Payload	**Key**	**Type**	**Example**
	Hash	string	\<sha 256 hash of this payload\>
	sender	string	\<pub key of sender\>
	signature	string	\<digital signature key of sender\>
	timestamp	string	1589135911
	Receiver	string	\<pub key of receiver\>
	Amount	int	\<amount of funcoins to send\>

Table 7-7. *peers payload*

Key	Value	
Name	Peers	
Payload	**Key**	**Type**
	Peers	List[peer]

Table 7-8. *block payload*

Key	Value	
Name	block	
Payload	**Key**	**Type**
	mined_by	string
	transactions	List[transaction]
	height	int
	difficulty	int
	hash	string
	previous_hash	string
	nonce	string
	timestamp	int

Using Marshmallow to validate our messages

We'll now use the marshmallow library to validate our messages. Our server performs two actions: reading messages and sending messages. When the server receives a message, that message arrives as a JSON string. It must then be transformed to a Python dictionary and validated; this process is called deserialization, since we're going from a serialized form (JSON) to a native Python dict. Serialization works the opposite: to go from a dict to a JSON string. In summary

1. Server reads messages being sent by peers (deserialize: json → dict).

2. Server sends messages to peers (serialize: dict → json).

For each object we want to validate, Marshmallow requires us to define a *schema*. Here's what the schema for a peer object looks like:

```
from marshmallow import Schema, fields

class Peer(Schema):
    ip = fields.Str(required=True)
    port = fields.Int(required=True)
    last_seen = fields.Int(missing=lambda: int(time()))
```

Notice that we specify the type of each field. When Marshmallow receives a JSON object, it will throw an error if one of the fields doesn't match their specified type, saving us a ton of time and effort. Here's an example of a serialized JSON string sent to our server:

```
payload = "{'ip': '192.168.0.1', 'port': 8888, 'last_seen':
1589780748}"
```

We can now ask Marshmallow to deserialize it:

```
result = Peer().loads(payload)
# <dict> {'last_seen': 1589780748, 'ip': '192.168.0.1',
'port': 8888}
```

If one of the fields were incorrect, or failed to validate, Marshmallow would go through a ValidationError.

Let's try serializing the result:

```
serialized = Peer().dumps(some_payload)
# "{'last_seen': 1589780748, 'ip': '192.168.0.1', 'port': 8888}"
```

If you're still unsure how Marshmallow works, or why it saves us a lot of hassle, it's worthwhile to check out the documentation, as they offer tons of examples on their website: https://marshmallow.readthedocs.io

---

Note   A common theme in most serialization libraries is to stick with loads and dumps as method names: loads deserializes from a string; load deserializes from an object; dumps serializes to a string; dump serializes to an object.

Implementing and validating types

Let's create three new files, funcoin/types.py, funcoin/messages.py, and funcoin/utils.py, to house our types, messages, and additional helper functions, respectively. Your folder structure should look like so:

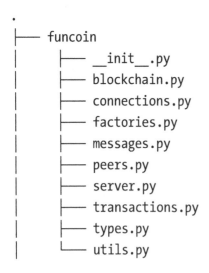

```
.
├── funcoin
│   ├── __init__.py
│   ├── blockchain.py
│   ├── connections.py
│   ├── factories.py
│   ├── messages.py
│   ├── peers.py
│   ├── server.py
│   ├── transactions.py
│   ├── types.py
│   └── utils.py
```

```
├───__init__.py
├─── node.py
├─── poetry.lock
└─── pyproject.toml
```

Let's first define the Marshmallow schema in funcoin/schema.py.

Listing 7-7. funcoin/schema.py

```
1   import json
2   from time import time
3
4   from marshmallow import Schema, fields, validates_schema,
    ValidationError
5
6
7   class Transaction(Schema):
8       timestamp = fields.Int()
9       sender = fields.Str()
10      receiver = fields.Str()
11      amount = fields.Int()
12      signature = fields.Str()
13
14      class Meta:
15          ordered = True
16
17
18  class Block(Schema):
19      mined_by = fields.Str(required=False)
20      transactions = fields.Nested(Transaction(), many=True)
21      height = fields.Int(required=True)
22      target = fields.Str(required=True)
23      hash = fields.Str(required=True)
```

```
24      previous_hash = fields.Str(required=True)
25      nonce = fields.Str(required=True)
26      timestamp = fields.Int(required=True)
27
28      class Meta:
29          ordered = True
30
31      @validates_schema
32      def validate_hash(self, data, **kwargs):
33          block = data.copy()
34          block.pop("hash")
35
36          if data["hash"] != json.dumps(block, sort_
            keys=True):
37              raise ValidationError("Fraudulent block: hash
                is wrong")
38
39
40  class Peer(Schema):
41      ip = fields.Str(required=True)
42      port = fields.Int(required=True)
43      last_seen = fields.Int(missing=lambda: int(time()))
```

In the code, we implement Peer, Block, and Transaction.

In Transaction, we include a validation method called validate_
signature. It is decorated with @validates_schema—a special decorator
indicating that Marshmallow should run this function as part of its
validation process. This is where we'll validate a transaction: at the point of
deserialization to ensure that *any* transaction we deserialize is *always* valid.

In Block, we too implement a validation method to ensure that any
block contained in *any* message is always valid.

Defining the messages (and their schema)

In funcoin/messages.py we'll implement the various messages and their schemas, then we'll test them to ensure they're consistent. These are the classes we'll be implementing:

- PeersMessage

- BlockMessage

- TransactionMessage

- PingPayload

- PingMessage

- Base

Note that the payload for PeersMessage is a list of Peer; the payload for BlockMessage is a Block, and the payload for TransactionMessage is a Transaction. This is why we defined them in types.py first.

As an exercise to the reader, you may want to skip ahead and try defining the schema for each message on your own.

Here's what they should look like when you're done.

Listing 7-8. funcoin/messages.py

```
1   from marshmallow import Schema, fields, post_load
2   from marshmallow_oneofschema import OneOfSchema
3
4   from funcoin.schema import Peer, Block, Transaction, Ping
5
6
7   class PeersMessage(Schema):
8       payload = fields.Nested(Peer(many=True))
9
10      @post_load
```

```
11        def add_name(self, data, **kwargs):
12            data["name"] = "peers"
13            return data
14
15
16  class BlockMessage(Schema):
17      payload = fields.Nested(Block)
18
19      @post_load
20      def add_name(self, data, **kwargs):
21          data["name"] = "block"
22          return data
23
24
25  class TransactionMessage(Schema):
26      payload = fields.Nested(Transaction)
27
28      @post_load
29      def add_name(self, data, **kwargs):
30          data["name"] = "transaction"
31          return data
32
33
34  class PingMessage(Schema):
35      payload = fields.Nested(Ping)
36
37      @post_load
38      def add_name(self, data, **kwargs):
39          data["name"] = "ping"
40          return data
41
42
```

```
43  class MessageDisambiguation(OneOfSchema):
44      type_field = "name"
45      type_schemas = {
46          "ping": PingMessage,
47          "peers": PeersMessage,
48          "block": BlockMessage,
49          "transaction": TransactionMessage,
50      }
51      def get_obj_type(self, obj):
52        if isinstance(obj, dict):
53            return obj.get("name")
54
55  class MetaSchema(Schema):
56      address = fields.Nested(Peer())
57      client = fields.Str()
58
59
60  class BaseSchema(Schema):
61      meta = fields.Nested(MetaSchema())
62      message = fields.Nested(MessageDisambiguation())
63
64
65  def meta(ip, port, version="funcoin-0.1"):
66      return {
67          "client": version,
68          "address": {
69              "ip": ip,
70              "port": port
71          },
72      }
73
74
```

```
75  def create_peers_message(external_ip,
    external_port, peers):
76      return BaseSchema().dumps({
77          "meta": meta(external_ip, external_port),
78          "message": {
79              "name": "peers",
80              "payload":  peers
81          }
82      }
83      )
84
85
86  def create_block_message(external_ip, external_port, block):
87      return BaseSchema().dumps({
88          "meta": meta(external_ip, external_port),
89          "message": {
90              "name": "block",
91              "payload": block
92          }
93      }
94      )
95
96  def create_transaction_message(external_ip, external_port, tx):
97      return BaseSchema().dumps(
98          {
99              "meta": meta(external_ip, external_port),
100             "message": {
101                 "name": "transaction",
102                 "payload": tx,
103             },
104         }
105     )
```

Note that we also include some helper functions to create the messages, for example, on line 89 we include create_block_message which generates a message containing a block. Let's test this given a block:

```
some_block = {
    "mined_by": "some public key",
    "transactions":    [],
    "height": 123,
    "difficulty": 10,
    "hash": "some fake hash", "previous_hash":   0,
    "nonce":   23,
    "timestamp":   238778621,
}
```

As you can see, this isn't a valid block; let's try loading this into the Block() validator:

```
Block().load(some_block)
```

```
marshmallow.exceptions.ValidationError: {'transactions':
{'_schema': ['Invalid input type.']}, 'previous_hash': ['Not a
valid string.'], 'nonce': ['Not a valid string.']}
```

As you can see, Marshmallow is pretty descriptive and tells us exactly what's wrong with the block. Let's try again, fixing the problems:

```
some_block = {
    "mined_by": "some public key",
    "transactions": [],
    "height": 123,
    "difficulty": 10,
    "hash": "some fake hash",
    "previous_hash":   0,
    "nonce":   23,
    "timestamp":   238778621,
}
```

```
Block().load(some_block)
```

```
ValidationError: {'_schema': ['Fraudulent block: hash is
wrong']}
```

As you can see, Marshmallow ran our validation function which correctly determined that our hash of "some fake hash" is obviously wrong. Let's try again:

```
some_block = {
    "mined_by": "some public key",
    "height": 123,
    "difficulty": 10,
    "previous_hash": "some previous hash",
    "nonce": "213",
    "timestamp": 238778621,
    "hash": "a52bfa60bc4ad3d3e9571eab8b28370166f2476e0f1026df
            219bec07a0a9e2e7"
}
```

```
# Passes validation by not throwing an exception
Block().load(some_block)
```

Now, we can use the helper method to generate a message:

```
from funcoin.messages import create_block_message
```

```
some_block = {
    "mined_by": "some public key",
    "height":  123,
    "difficulty": 10,
    "previous_hash": "some previous hash",
    "nonce":  "213",
```

```
    "timestamp": 238778621,
    "hash": "a52bfa60bc4ad3d3e9571eab8b28370166f2476e0f1026df
            219bec07a0a9e2e7"
}
message = create_block_message(some_block, "127.0.0.1", 8888)
```

Now we can send message to our peers, and thus complete fleshing out the funcoin/peers.py module.

Bringing it all together

Before we can run our node, there's still a bit more handiwork to be done:

1. We need to find a way of locating our external IP address, this is the IP address that is visible to the outside world.

2. Find a way of "bootstrapping" peers to our node when it boots up: after all, we need to populate a network.

3. Decide if our node is to be a miner; if so, we'll need to instruct it to begin mining (and propagating blocks to our peers when one is found).

Let's address the given points sequentially.

Finding your external IP address

There are third-party services which, when you connect to them, will divulge your external IP address. This may sound strange, but this is actually how Bitcoin nodes find their own external IP addresses.

Open up your terminal, and let's use cURL to hit the ipinfo.io service:

```
curl ipinfo.io
{
  "ip": "72.81.18.117",
  "hostname":  "XX-XX-XXX-XXX.com",
  "city":  "New  York  City",
  "region":  "New  York",
  "country": "US",
  "loc": "41.5143,-73.8060",
  "org": "AS701 MCI Communications Services, Inc. d/b/a Verizon
          Business",
  "postal": "10004",
  "timezone": "America/New_York",
  "readme": "https://ipinfo.io/missingauth"
}
```

Note that it shows me what my external ip is (72.81.18.117). Let's write a method to do this in Python when our node boots up in funcoin/utils.py:

```
import aiohttp
import structlog

logger = structlog.getLogger(__name__)

async def get_external_ip():
    async with aiohttp.ClientSession() as session:
        async with session.get('http://ipinfo.io',
        headers={"user-agent": "curl/7.64.1"}) as response:
            response_json = await response.json(content_
            type=None)
            ip = response_json["ip"]
            logger.info(f"Found external IP: {ip}")
            return ip
```

When we run the `listen()` method of our server in `server.py`, we can populate the IP address.

Listing 7-9. funcoin/server.py

```
1  async def listen(self, hostname="0.0.0.0", port=8888):
2      server = await asyncio.start_server(self.handle_
       connection, hostname, port)
3      logger.info(f"Server listening on {hostname}:{port}")
4
5      self.external_ip = await self.get_external_ip()
6      self.external_port = 8888
7
8      async with server:
9          await server.serve_forever()
```

Let's try loading our server for the first time:

```
(venv) $ python node.py
2020-05-18  02:42.28 Creating genesis block
2020-05-18 02:42.28 Server listening on 0.0.0.0:8888
2020-05-18 02:42.28 Found external IP: 72.81.18.117
```

Woah, how awesome is that? Our server is now running on the network. But peers won't be able to connect to us for a couple of reasons:

1. You have a firewall enabled (and unless you really know what you're doing, you should keep it enabled).

2. Your Wi-Fi router/access point does not forward outside connections to your local computer (where you're probably running this), and nor should it (it's a major security vulnerability).

3. Peers on the network have no way of finding us because we're the only node so far.

Note   The preceding reasons should paint a stark picture of how difficult building a p2p network really is; besides the security problems of opening up incoming Internet traffic, it's also really difficult to seed a network of always-online peers. If you're serious about testing one, I suggest paying a few dollars a month for an AWS EC2 or DigitalOcean Droplets (recommended) and running a node in a context where there's little risk in being attacked.

## CHAPTER 8

Comparisons to Real-World Decentralized Networks

Congratulations, you've got a working node (and you're a funcoinaire). But how different is it to Bitcoin? Or Ethereum? Or Monero? Or any of the flavors out there? What alternatives are there to Proof of Work? What are smart contracts? In this chapter we'll explore the differences between funcoin and real production blockchains and try to quantify the distance between them.

Why blockchain engineering is hard

Blockchain engineering gives rise to some of the hardest problems in the realm of computer science mainly because they are decentralized: they link together concepts from distributed systems, networking, concurrency, cryptography, economics, and game theory. And any work done to fix bugs or shortcomings must happen in the context of a live system without sacrificing usability. To compound this, any client with fresh software must still maintain the ability to validate blocks created by the old software, creating an ever-expanding list of *if* statements—it's akin to fixing problems on a jumbo jet while the jet is in mid-flight and loaded with passengers.

© Daniel van Flymen 2020
D. van Flymen, *Learn Blockchain by Building One*,
https://doi.org/10.1007/978-1-4842-5171-3_8

Behind open source software is the idea that fixes and changes are contributed by anybody interested. Bitcoin is interesting from a game theoretical point of view because over time, as more wealth is invested into it, the ever-watchful eyes of the invested should be able to react faster to threats and fixes. But there are certainly not as many applications that place such a heightened importance on backward compatibility as Bitcoin. Since a single mistake could cause all that wealth (at the time of writing, $120 billion dollars) to disappear, Bitcoin's philosophy is to tread carefully and gain the consensus of the dev community before doubling down on things, quadruple-checking them once more for good measure before merging them. And in some circumstances, bugs just aren't worth fixing since the cost of the fix simply isn't worth the hassle of the upgrade. As an example, in Bitcoin, Satoshi himself introduced the well-known time warp bug which causes blocks to always be mined slightly short of 10 minutes (instead of 10 minutes): instead of averaging the time spent mining the last 2016 blocks, the algorithm is off by one and looks at the last 2015 blocks. This means that blocks are slightly more difficult to mine than they should be. It's not considered a major problem, but the cost of fixing it well outweighs the benefits.

In public blockchains, changes arrive in one of two flavors: hard forks and soft forks. Hard forks are divergences from the current block chain. This makes old clients no longer able to understand the new protocol followed by new clients. Bitcoin Cash, Bitcoin Gold, Bitcoin XT, and Bitcoin Classic are all examples of hard forks of Bitcoin. On the other hand, soft forks are backward-compatible: new blocks, generated by new clients, are able to be validated by old clients.

Not to be confused with hard fork (a change in consensus rules that breaks security for nodes that don't upgrade), soft fork (a change in consensus rules that weakens security for nodes that don't upgrade), software fork (when one or more developers permanently develops a codebase separately from other developers), and git fork (when one or more developers temporarily develops a codebase separately from other developers).

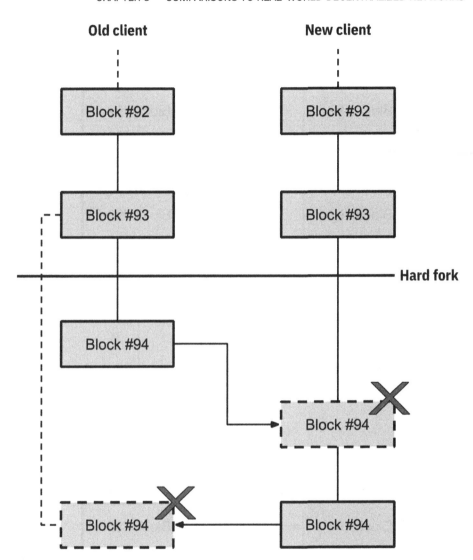

Figure 8-1. *A hard fork*

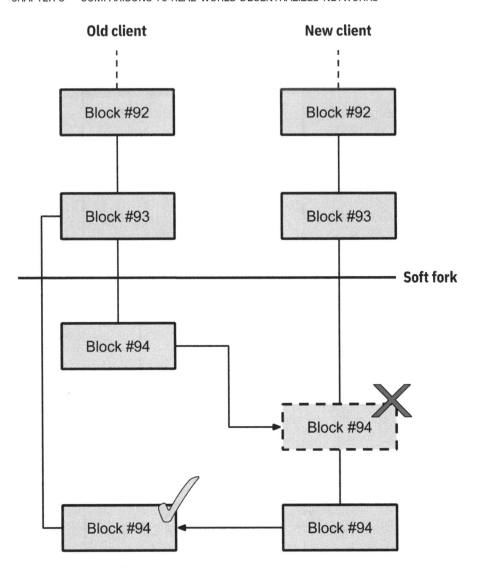

Figure 8-2. *A soft fork*

Note   Another type of fork is a software fork, since codebases are open sourced, nothing is preventing you from "forking" Bitcoin's codebase into your own. There are plenty of projects that regularly do this, the most notable of which is Litecoin.

The shortcomings of funcoin

As you've experienced firsthand, there are roughly four critical components needed in order to have a *publicly* functioning blockchain:

- A **consensus protocol** which allows distributed peers to agree on the state of the system (the data stored in the blockchain). It's this magic that allows us to call a blockchain "decentralized."

- A **networking layer** which allows peers to communicate and propagate information throughout the network.

- A **chain of cryptographically secured blocks** (the blockchain itself).

- An **economical incentivization scheme** (proof of work) which secures the chain under the pressure of work.

Problems arising in any of these components almost always have implications for *all* of them. For example, a bug in the networking layer may be exploited to delay the propagation of transactions to certain nodes on the network, thereby affecting the consensus protocol. Writing this book has been extremely tricky for me because I set out to build an easy-to-understand blockchain that would be simple to understand, only to come to the slow realization that projects like Bitcoin have the same goal: in some sense, they *are* the simplest manifestation of their protocols.

As a mental exercise, I'd like you to take a moment and reflect on the work done in the various components of funcoin and think about how resilient they are to attack. The network layer is a difficult and complex facet of our system; that's probably a good place to start.

The networking layer

The first assumption we made in the network layer was to use JSON as a serialization format for our messages. This is suboptimal for a myriad of reasons, mostly because it does not support streaming. In other words, we need to know where one JSON-encoded object starts and another begins. In order to get around this hurdle, we made the rule that messages are delimited by newlines. Here's the code in our Server class that accomplishes this:

```
1   async def handle_connection(self, reader: StreamReader,
    writer: StreamWriter):
2       while True:
3           try:
4               # Wait forever on new data to arrive
5               data = await reader.readuntil(b"\n")
6
7               decoded_data = data.decode("utf8").strip()
8
9               try:
10                  message = BaseSchema().loads(decoded_data)
11              except  MarshmallowError:
```

```
12              logger.info("Received unreadable message",
                peer=writer)
13              break
14
15          # Extract the address from the message, add it
              to the writer object
16          writer.address = message["meta"]["address"]
17
18          # Let's add the peer to our connection pool
19          self.connection_pool.add_peer(writer)
20
21          # ...and handle the message
22          await self.p2p_protocol.handle_message
              (message, writer)
23
24          await writer.drain()
25          if writer.is_closing():
26              break
27
28      except (asyncio.exceptions.IncompleteReadError,
        ConnectionError):
29          # An error happened, break out of the wait loop
30          break
```

Can you see the problem with this? It leaves our node open to a denial of service attack. All somebody needs to do is send us a message without a newline, and our node would keep the connection open, waiting for the message to end. This, however, can be easily mitigated by keeping track and throttling the amount of data a peer may send us. That being said, we used JSON-based messages to make the implementation easier. Bitcoin uses column-delimited bytes for message structures, which would require arduous implementation. Here's the structure of a Bitcoin message:

Field Size	Description	Data Type	Comments
4	magic	uint32	Signifies if the message should be on test or real network
12	command	char[12]	String signifying the message's content type
4	length	uint32	Size in bytes of the payload
4	checksum	uint32	The first 4 bytes of the hash of the message
?	payload	char[]	The actual data

We also have not spoken about how our node sorts and stores peers. We have no heuristic for doing so. Let me give you an example of what I mean by a *heuristic*: when a peer asks us for nodes, we could send them *all* the nodes we know about, but that's wasteful and could be better considered. What if we sent the requesting node 20 peers at random? Would that result in a peer being able to propagate a transaction to the entire network (assuming other peers also returned random nodes)? This is largely in the realm of peer-to-peer research, and such heuristics are typically called *Gossip Protocols* or *Peer Discovery*. This area of research garnered renewed interest after the famous shutdown of Napster—the first software allowing people to download music from a peer-to-peer network. But Napster was centralized: it served a list of available peers, and so if Napster went down, so did the network.

BitTorrent is an example of a distributed hash table (DHT): a decentralized key value storage system typically used to download movies and TV shows illegally via websites like The Pirate Bay and ISOHunt.

Governments and law enforcement agencies for years tried to shut down these so-called torrent websites but were largely unsuccessful—they still exist today. But why? What makes them so resilient to censorship? It seems like blockchains such as Bitcoin and Ethereum should learn a thing or two from DHTs like eDonkey and Kad. The secret lies in how nodes on these networks discover and organize their peers—doing it correctly makes a P2P network scalable, censorship-resistant, and fast. If your network needs to support file storage, you may consider using a DHT, since they are really just rules for governing which nodes on the network host which files. If you're building a decentralized blockchain, you don't need to worry about storing large files, since everybody is really storing the same "large" file— the blockchain itself.

Most of the research around peer-to-peer protocols is nascent, and comes from file sharing. Modern decentralized networks exist at the application layer, and implement protocols for

- **Peer Discovery**: How to discover nodes on the network

- **Routing**: Which routes to take to contact nodes (messages)

- **Naming**: A uniform way to identify nodes

These protocols almost always exist at the Application Layer of the networking stack.

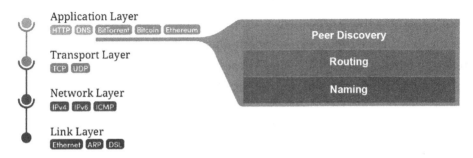

Figure 8-3. *The typical network stack*

Peer Discovery

Modern peer-to-peer networks aren't centralized: There was a time when they were—when BitTorrent used trackers (servers that list tons of IPs to connect to, like Napster). But if peer-to-peer networks relied on trackers, they'd be susceptible to an easy form of attack: bringing down the tracker.

Imagine you and I want to talk to each other over the Internet, without a server. How do we find each other's IPs?

> Let's use email/SMS/Telegram/WhatsApp to send
> our IPs to each-other?

That could work, but it's **centralized**—if email is down, the system doesn't work (interestingly, Bitcoin used IRC Chatrooms to list IPs in the early days).

> We can agree to run our clients on a specific port
> and keep pinging random IPs on that port until we
> find each other.

Finding each other is unlikely—we'd have to ping approximately 232-1 IPV4 and an unimaginable 2^{128}-1 IPv6 addresses. **But that's on the right track!**

> So, how does Bitcoin do it?

It turns out that if the network is large enough, we can use a combination of those previously presented: When a Bitcoin client is started for the first time, it doesn't know about the world, or any other nodes—it relies on hard-coded DNS entries. These DNS entries are maintained by the Bitcoin community and return lists of trusted addresses for the client to connect to.

But DNS servers are centralized: A single server can be spoofed and made to return phony IP addresses, isolating a node to accept fake transactions and a bogus blockchain. For this reason alone, clients shouldn't rely solely on DNS. Thus, there's an inherent risk when running a client for the first time, but it's mitigated by the fact that the longer a client is running, the more costly it is to maintain an attack.

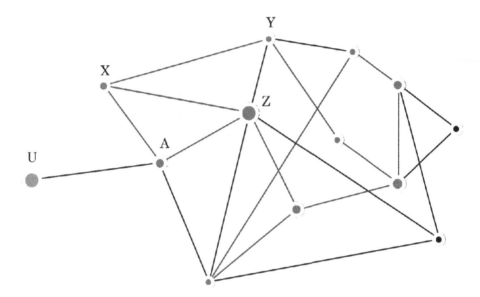

Figure 8-4. *A node joining a network for the first time*

In the preceding diagram, when our Bitcoin client node U finds another node, it starts communicating with it:

Hello node A, I'm using Bitcoin protocol v0.16.0

node A then responds:

Hey node U! I'm also using v0.16.0, my latest block is 528491, and here are some other nodes I know about: node X, node Z, ...

node A then broadcasts us to other nodes who may contact us too. And we can download missing blocks from our new *swarm* of nodes and ask them for information about their neighbors too.

This is the basis of peer discovery, and why P2P networks are resilient—there's no central point of failure, just a "cloud" of nodes. And stopping a well-organized network is akin to censoring individual network connections—an infeasible task.

Naming

The IP address of a peer can change, so we need a way of consistently referring to it on the network. Ethereum uses a 256-bit hash of a peer's public key to identify a peer. BitTorrent uses 160-bit hash of a random number. In any case, identifiers are large enough to guarantee uniqueness. If the network uses an appropriate hash function, say SHA-256, then we can allow for ~2256 peers on our network.

Distance functions

Before we can organize our network, we need a way to measure the "distance" between two peers on a network. In mathematics, this is called a metric. It means "a way to measure distance." It's important to understand that we are not referring to geographical (Euclidean) distance, we're talking about something abstract, a common way of the network deciding how close two nodes are from each other.

In 2002, two researchers Petar Maymounkov and David Mazières published a groundbreaking paper called Kademlia. It describes how, when providing a specific way of measuring distance, a decentralized network can be structured in such a way that it becomes fast, resilient, and routable. Most DHTs, like BitTorrent, adopted the Kademlia algorithm. Let's talk a bit about how it works.

The Kademlia algorithm uses the XOR (Exclusive or) function to measure the distance between any two nodes. As a refresh, XOR is a logical operation between two inputs which outputs true only when the two inputs are different. Here are some examples:

```
1000 XOR 1000 = 0000

0000 XOR 1111 = 1111

1011 XOR 0101 = 1110
```

In mathematics, to be called a metric, a distance function must satisfy the following three criteria (as the XOR metric indeed does):

- The distance between a node and itself is zero.

- The distance between node A and node B is the same as the distance between node B and node A (symmetry).

- The distance from node A to node B to node C is always greater than or equal to the distance from node A to node C (the triangle inequality).

Furthermore, the XOR function is trivial to implement and cheap to calculate. It's important to realize that the XOR function simply calculates the distance between two node IDs.

Routing

The following image shows the network map for a small network with a maximum of eight nodes. The node IDs are listed as leaves along the bottom of the diagram. The image shows how the network is structured as seen from the view of node 110. As you can see, the closest node is 111 since 110 XOR 111 = 001. The furthest node is 001 since 110 XOR 001 = 111. As you can see, there are a few great properties about using XOR as a distance function; firstly it guarantees that half the network is stored in the farthest collection (or bucket as it's referred to in the paper). This is convenient because then if a peer asks node 110 for its neighbors, 110 needs only to return the closest peers to the requesting node.

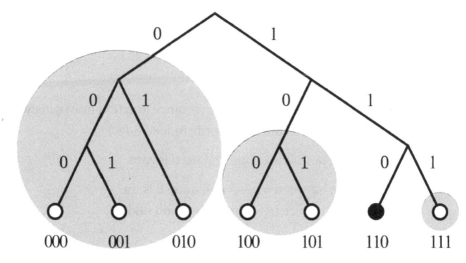

Figure 8-5. *The Kademlia algorithm*

Data persistence

Our blockchain is stored in memory, that is, our `Blockchain` class clears and maintains the entire chain in the running program!

```
class  Blockchain(object):
    def __init__(self):
        self.chain = []
```

This means that every time we restart the server, our node will have to download the entire blockchain from its neighbors. The blockchain is monotonic—it is ever-increasing in size—so we'll need to find a better solution for storing it. Bitcoin uses Google's LevelDB database for local storage. LevelDB is a simple key value store that can be persisted to disk. At the time of writing, Bitcoin's full storage space is around 160GB.

Alternative consensus: Proof of stake

Throughout this book we've only spoken about proof of work: the algorithm which secures our blockchain and creates consensus. It's worth mentioning that there are loud criticisms against proof of work, the most popular of which is the argument that it is bad for the environment: it's no secret that Bitcoin consumes an enormous amount of energy for proof of work. But this is largely contested by a game theoretical argument that it's precisely this energy which secures the network. Additionally, it incentivizes Bitcoin miners to stay profitable by moving their mining operations to states which have electricity surpluses or low-cost renewable energy. At the macro level, Bitcoin maximalists contrast the energy usage to the indeterminable costs of running a fiat banking system with countless branches, vaults, electricity, employees, forms, and a seemingly endless supply of paper notes.

In Proof of Stake (PoS), the miner of the next block is *chosen* by an algorithm according to certain criteria. Depending on the implementation, these criteria may be related to the miner's wealth or period of time that they've maintained a balance or be completely at random. In contrast, PoS does not require an abundant usage of energy to secure the network. NXT is a cryptocurrency that has implemented pure Proof of Stake; other cryptocurrencies like Peercoin use a hybrid system, while (at the time of writing) Ethereum has been in the process of moving toward a PoS system.

There are plenty of developers in the community who don't see Proof of Stake as an ideal replacement for proof of work due to a variety of factors. The first is that proof of work offers additional network layer benefits: if Bitcoin had to suffer an eclipse attack—tons of bad actor nodes on the network attempting to facade an alternative chain—those actors would be forced to repeat *all* the work done with the trillions of terawatt-hours of electricity, making it infeasible; the second is that Proof of Stake is susceptible to a problem known as the *nothing-at-stake* problem wherein miners (perhaps a better term is block generators) have nothing

157

to lose by acting in bad faith (voting for multiple blockchain histories) and preventing consensus. This is a direct consequence of having no sunk economic cost (like energy), so there is no cost to working on multiple chains at once. In order to mitigate these vulnerabilities, punitive protocols have been suggested which punish bad actors on the network.

Smart contracts

The idea of a "smart" contract was originally introduced by Bitcoin's P2PK (Pay to Pubkey) and P2PH (Pay to Pubkey Hash). Ethereum breakthrough was the introduction of Turing-complete language to write smart contracts. In lay terms, Turing completeness means that the smart contract language can effectively compute operations like any real-world computer.

The introduction of smart contracts was initially seen as a more comprehensive version of Bitcoin's Script system or, more simply, code that can be stored on the blockchain and executed by miners. It's called a *contract* because the idea behind the code is that it operates against accounts or serves as an intermediary logging events in the blockchain or taking action when certain criteria are met. This is pertinent in the legal space as it alleviates the need for middlemen or intermediaries. In funcoin, our blockchain stores simple transactions, not instructions (or code). Technically, a smart contract is not that smart at all—it's a bunch of code, written in a special language that miners (and nodes) run when they validate a block. This code may instruct funds to be transferred from one account to another or allow a certain transaction to happen upon request; the possibilities are seemingly endless.

> *Example 1. Notarizing a Document*
>
> Let's say that you wanted to notarize a document. You'd first need to instruct your bank to pay your lawyer and then wait for your lawyer to process your document. With a smart contract, however, there's

no need for banks or any intermediation. With smart contracts, the lawyer can be paid automatically once they produce a document satisfying certain conditions set by your code.

Example 2. Buying a house

Buying a property is a very complicated procedure. There are typically commission-based brokers, representing the seller and buyer. They coordinate with each other and with their respective lawyers and banks to manage the taxable process. In certain cases, money must also be placed in an escrow account to release the funds from the buyer to the seller when all the paperwork has been complete. This process places a hefty amount of *trust* in many places to facilitate what in essence is a simple transaction. In this case, a smart contract can automatically act as both escrow service and payment provider—since all parties can be transacted with *automatically* when criteria are met.

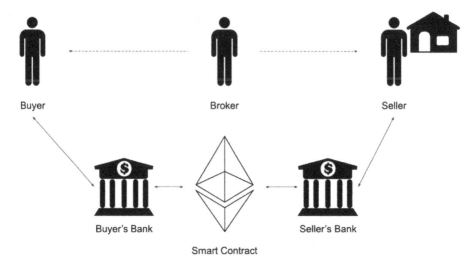

Figure 8-6. *A smart contract example*

Example 3. ICOs (Initial Coin Offerings)

ICOs can be thought of as blockchain-based crowdfunding. If you'd like to sell shares in your new project or company, you can create a smart contract which grants somebody a share when they transfer coins to a specific account. These shares are usually in the form of tokens.

What does a smart contract look like?

In Ethereum, smart contracts are written in a language called Solidity. Here is an example of a voting contract (from the Solidity documentation at https://github.com/ethereum/solidity/blob/v0.4.20/docs/solidity-by-example.rst):

```
/// @title Voting with delegation.
```

```
contract Ballot {
    // This declares a new complex type which will
    // be used for variables later.
    // It will represent a single voter.
    struct Voter {
        uint weight; // weight is accumulated by delegation
        bool voted;  // if true, that person already voted
        address delegate; // person delegated to
        uint vote; // index of the voted proposal
    }

    // This is a type for a single proposal.
    struct Proposal {
        bytes32 name;   // short name (up to 32 bytes)
        uint voteCount; // number of accumulated votes
    }

    address public chairperson;

    // This declares a state variable that
    // stores a `Voter` struct for each possible address.
    mapping(address => Voter) public voters;

    // A dynamically sized array of `Proposal` structs.
    Proposal[] public proposals;

    /// Create a new ballot to choose one of `proposalNames`.
    constructor(bytes32[] memory proposalNames) public {
        chairperson = msg.sender;
        voters[chairperson].weight = 1;

        // For each of the provided proposal names,
        // create a new proposal object and add it
        // to the end of the array.
```

```
    for (uint i = 0; i < proposalNames.length; i++) {
        // `Proposal({...})` creates a temporary
        // Proposal object and `proposals.push(...)`
        // appends it to the end of `proposals`.
        proposals.push(Proposal({
            name:  proposalNames[i],
            voteCount: 0
        }));
    }
}

// Give `voter` the right to vote on this ballot.
// May only be called by `chairperson`.
function giveRightToVote(address voter) public {
    // If the first argument of `require` evaluates
    // to `false`, execution terminates, and all
    // changes to the state and to Ether balances
    // are reverted.
    // This used to consume all gas in old EVM versions but
    // not anymore.
    // It is often a good idea to use `require` to check if
    // functions are called correctly.
    // As a second argument, you can also provide an
    // explanation about what went wrong.
    require(
        msg.sender == chairperson,
        "Only chairperson can give right to vote."
    );
    require(
        !voters[voter].voted,
        "The voter already voted."
    );
```

```solidity
    require(voters[voter].weight == 0);
    voters[voter].weight = 1;
}

/// Delegate your vote to the voter `to`.
function delegate(address to) public {
    // assigns reference
    Voter storage sender = voters[msg.sender];
    require(!sender.voted, "You already voted.");

    require(to != msg.sender, "Self-delegation is
    disallowed.");

    // Forward the delegation as long as
    // `to` is also delegated.
    // In general, such loops are very dangerous,
    // because if they run too long, they might
    // need more gas than is available in a block.
    // In this case, the delegation will not be executed,
    // but in other situations, such loops might
    // cause a contract to get "stuck" completely.
    while (voters[to].delegate != address(0)) {
        to = voters[to].delegate;

        // We found a loop in the delegation, not allowed.
        require(to != msg.sender, "Found loop in
        delegation.");
    }

    // Since `sender` is a reference, this
    // modifies `voters[msg.sender].voted`
    sender.voted = true;
    sender.delegate = to;
    Voter storage delegate_ = voters[to];
```

```
    if (delegate_.voted) {
        // If the delegate already voted,
        // directly add to the number of votes
        proposals[delegate_.vote].voteCount  +=  sender.
        weight;
    } else {
        // If the delegate did not vote yet,
        // add to her weight.
        delegate_.weight  +=  sender.weight;
    }
}

/// Give your vote (including votes delegated to you)
/// to proposal `proposals[proposal].name`.
function vote(uint proposal) public {
    Voter storage sender = voters[msg.sender];
    require(sender.weight != 0, "Has no right to vote");
    require(!sender.voted, "Already voted.");
    sender.voted = true;
    sender.vote = proposal;

    // If `proposal` is out of the range of the array,
    // this will throw automatically and revert all
    // changes.
    proposals[proposal].voteCount += sender.weight;
}

/// @dev Computes the winning proposal taking all
/// previous votes into account.
function winningProposal() public view
        returns (uint winningProposal_)
```

```
{
    uint winningVoteCount = 0;
    for (uint p = 0; p < proposals.length; p++) {
        if (proposals[p].voteCount > winningVoteCount) {
            winningVoteCount = proposals[p].voteCount;
            winningProposal_ = p;
        }
    }
}

// Calls winningProposal() function to get the index
// of the winner contained in the proposals array and then
// returns the name of the winner
function winnerName() public view
        returns (bytes32 winnerName_)
{
    winnerName_ = proposals[winningProposal()].name;
}
}
```

When this code is executed by a miner, the computation is measured in *gas*. In other words, *gas* is a calculation of the amount of computational effort to execute the contract. Every operation costs some amount of gas, and miners are paid by fees (in Ether) for the total amount of gas they spent. This economy incentivizes contracts to be written efficiently.

Bitcoin: A Peer-to-Peer Electronic Cash System by Satoshi Nakamoto

This is the original whitepaper, reproduced in its entirety as published by Satoshi Nakamoto on October 31, 2008.

Abstract

A purely peer-to-peer version of electronic cash would allow online payments to be sent directly from one party to another without going through a financial institution. Digital signatures provide part of the solution, but the main benefits are lost if a trusted third party is still required to prevent double-spending. We propose a solution to the double-spending problem using a peer-to-peer network. The network timestamps transactions by hashing them into an ongoing chain of hash-based proof-of-work, forming a record that cannot be changed without redoing the proof-of-work. The longest chain not only serves as proof of the sequence of events witnessed, but proof that it came from the largest

© Daniel van Flymen 2020
D. van Flymen, *Learn Blockchain by Building One*,
https://doi.org/10.1007/978-1-4842-5171-3

pool of CPU power. As long as a majority of CPU power is controlled by nodes that are not cooperating to attack the network, they'll generate the longest chain and outpace attackers. The network itself requires minimal structure. Messages are broadcast on a best effort basis, and nodes can leave and rejoin the network at will, accepting the longest proof-of-work chain as proof of what happened while they were gone.

Introduction

Commerce on the Internet has come to rely almost exclusively on financial institutions serving as trusted third parties to process electronic payments. While the system works well enough for most transactions, it still suffers from the inherent weaknesses of the trust based model. Completely non-reversible transactions are not really possible, since financial institutions cannot avoid mediating disputes. The cost of mediation increases transaction costs, limiting the minimum practical transaction size and cutting off the possibility for small casual transactions, and there is a broader cost in the loss of ability to make non-reversible payments for non-reversible services. With the possibility of reversal, the need for trust spreads. Merchants must be wary of their customers, hassling them for more information than they would otherwise need. A certain percentage of fraud is accepted as unavoidable. These costs and payment uncertainties can be avoided in person by using physical currency, but no mechanism exists to make payments over a communications channel without a trusted party.

What is needed is an electronic payment system based on cryptographic proof instead of trust, allowing any two willing parties to transact directly with each other without the need for a trusted third party. Transactions that are computationally impractical to reverse would protect sellers from fraud, and routine escrow mechanisms could easily be implemented to protect buyers. In this paper, we propose a solution to the double-spending problem using a peer-to-peer distributed timestamp server to generate computational proof of the chronological order of transactions. The system is secure as long as honest nodes collectively control more CPU power than any cooperating group of attacker nodes.

Transactions

We define an electronic coin as a chain of digital signatures. Each owner transfers the coin to the next by digitally signing a hash of the previous transaction and the public key of the next owner and adding these to the end of the coin. A payee can verify the signatures to verify the chain of ownership.

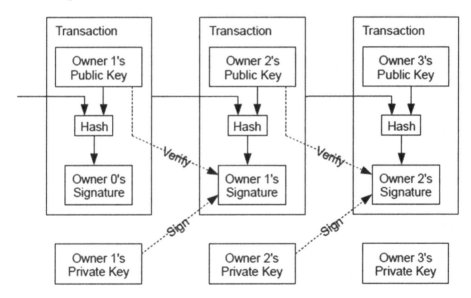

The problem of course is the payee can't verify that one of the owners did not double-spend the coin. A common solution is to introduce a trusted central authority, or mint, that checks every transaction for double spending. After each transaction, the coin must be returned to the mint to issue a new coin, and only coins issued directly from the mint are trusted not to be double-spent. The problem with this solution is that the fate of the entire money system depends on the company running the mint, with every transaction having to go through them, just like a bank.

We need a way for the payee to know that the previous owners did not sign any earlier transactions. For our purposes, the earliest transaction is the one that counts, so we don't care about later attempts to double-spend. The only way to confirm the absence of a transaction is to be aware of all transactions. In the mint based model, the mint was aware of all transactions and decided which arrived first. To accomplish this without a trusted party, transactions must be publicly announced [1], and we need a system for participants to agree on a single history of the order in which they were received. The payee needs proof that at the time of each transaction, the majority of nodes agreed it was the first received.

Timestamp Server

The solution we propose begins with a timestamp server. A timestamp server works by taking a hash of a block of items to be timestamped and widely publishing the hash, such as in a newspaper or Usenet post [2-5]. The timestamp proves that the data must have existed at the time, obviously, in order to get into the hash. Each timestamp includes the previous timestamp in its hash, forming a chain, with each additional timestamp reinforcing the ones before it.

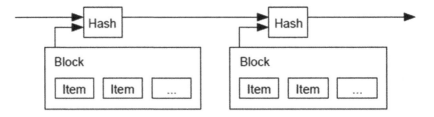

Proof-of-Work

To implement a distributed timestamp server on a peer-to-peer basis, we will need to use a proof-of-work system similar to Adam Back's Hashcash [6], rather than newspaper or Usenet posts. The proof-of-work involves scanning for a value that when hashed, such as with SHA-256, the hash begins with a number of zero bits. The average work required is exponential in the number of zero bits required and can be verified by executing a single hash.

For our timestamp network, we implement the proof-of-work by incrementing a nonce in the block until a value is found that gives the block's hash the required zero bits. Once the CPU effort has been expended to make it satisfy the proof-of-work, the block cannot be changed without redoing the work. As later blocks are chained after it, the work to change the block would include redoing all the blocks after it.

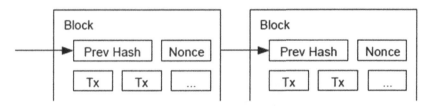

The proof-of-work also solves the problem of determining representation in majority decision making. If the majority were based on one-IP-address-one-vote, it could be subverted by anyone able to allocate many IPs. Proof-of-work is essentially one-CPU-one-vote. The majority decision is represented by the longest chain, which has the greatest proof-of-work effort invested in it. If a majority of CPU power is controlled by honest nodes, the honest chain will grow the fastest and outpace any competing chains. To modify a past block, an attacker would have to redo the proof-of-work of the block and all blocks after it and then catch up with and surpass the work of the honest nodes. We will show later that the probability of a slower attacker catching up diminishes exponentially as subsequent blocks are added.

To compensate for increasing hardware speed and varying interest in running nodes over time, the proof-of-work difficulty is determined by a moving average targeting an average number of blocks per hour. If they're generated too fast, the difficulty increases.

Network

The steps to run the network are as follows:

1. New transactions are broadcast to all nodes.

2. Each node collects new transactions into a block.

3. Each node works on finding a difficult proof-of-work for its block.

4. When a node finds a proof-of-work, it broadcasts the block to all nodes.

5. Nodes accept the block only if all transactions in it are valid and not already spent.

6. Nodes express their acceptance of the block by working on creating the next block in the chain, using the hash of the accepted block as the previous hash.

Nodes always consider the longest chain to be the correct one and will keep working on extending it. If two nodes broadcast different versions of the next block simultaneously, some nodes may receive one or the other first. In that case, they work on the first one they received, but save the other branch in case it becomes longer. The tie will be broken when the next proof-of-work is found and one branch becomes longer; the nodes that were working on the other branch will then switch to the longer one.

New transaction broadcasts do not necessarily need to reach all nodes. As long as they reach many nodes, they will get into a block before long. Block broadcasts are also tolerant of dropped messages. If a node does not receive a block, it will request it when it receives the next block and realizes it missed one.

Incentive

By convention, the first transaction in a block is a special transaction that starts a new coin owned by the creator of the block. This adds an incentive for nodes to support the network, and provides a way to initially distribute coins into circulation, since there is no central authority to issue them. The steady addition of a constant of amount of new coins is analogous to gold miners expending resources to add gold to circulation. In our case, it is CPU time and electricity that is expended.

The incentive can also be funded with transaction fees. If the output value of a transaction is less than its input value, the difference is a transaction fee that is added to the incentive value of the block containing the transaction. Once a predetermined number of coins have entered circulation, the incentive can transition entirely to transaction fees and be completely inflation free.

The incentive may help encourage nodes to stay honest. If a greedy attacker is able to assemble more CPU power than all the honest nodes, he would have to choose between using it to defraud people by stealing back his payments, or using it to generate new coins. He ought to find it more profitable to play by the rules, such rules that favor him with more new coins than everyone else combined, than to undermine the system and the validity of his own wealth.

Reclaiming Disk Space

Once the latest transaction in a coin is buried under enough blocks, the spent transactions before it can be discarded to save disk space. To facilitate this without breaking the block's hash, transactions are hashed in a Merkle Tree [7][2][5], with only the root included in the block's hash. Old blocks can then be compacted by stubbing off branches of the tree. The interior hashes do not need to be stored.

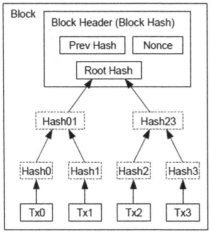

Transactions Hashed in a Merkle Tree   After Pruning Tx0-2 from the Block

A block header with no transactions would be about 80 bytes. If we suppose blocks are generated every 10 minutes, 80 bytes * 6 * 24 * 365 = 4.2MB per year. With computer systems typically selling with 2GB of RAM as of 2008, and Moore's Law predicting current growth of 1.2GB per year, storage should not be a problem even if the block headers must be kept in memory.

Simplified Payment Verification

It is possible to verify payments without running a full network node. A user only needs to keep a copy of the block headers of the longest proof-of-work chain, which he can get by querying network nodes until he's convinced he has the longest chain, and obtain the Merkle branch linking the transaction to the block it's timestamped in. He can't check the transaction for himself, but by linking it to a place in the chain, he can see that a network node has accepted it, and blocks added after it further confirm the network has accepted it.

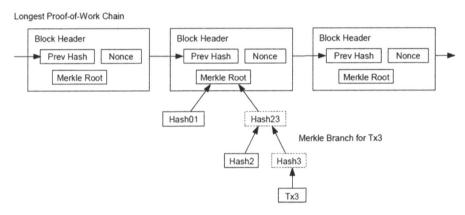

As such, the verification is reliable as long as honest nodes control the network, but is more vulnerable if the network is overpowered by an attacker. While network nodes can verify transactions for themselves, the simplified method can be fooled by an attacker's fabricated transactions for as long as the attacker can continue to overpower the network. One strategy to protect against this would be to accept alerts from network nodes when they detect an invalid block, prompting the user's software to download the full block and alerted transactions to confirm the inconsistency. Businesses that receive frequent payments will probably still want to run their own nodes for more independent security and quicker verification.

Combining and Splitting Value

Although it would be possible to handle coins individually, it would be unwieldy to make a separate transaction for every cent in a transfer. To allow value to be split and combined, transactions contain multiple inputs and outputs. Normally there will be either a single input from a larger previous transaction or multiple inputs combining smaller amounts, and at most two outputs: one for the payment, and one returning the change, if any, back to the sender.

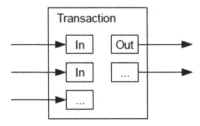

It should be noted that fan-out, where a transaction depends on several transactions, and those transactions depend on many more, is not a problem here. There is never the need to extract a complete standalone copy of a transaction's history.

Privacy

The traditional banking model achieves a level of privacy by limiting access to information to the parties involved and the trusted third party. The necessity to announce all transactions publicly precludes this method, but privacy can still be maintained by breaking the flow of information in another place: by keeping public keys anonymous. The public can see that someone is sending an amount to someone else, but without information linking the transaction to anyone. This is similar to the level of information released by stock exchanges, where the time and size of individual trades, the "tape", is made public, but without telling who the parties were.

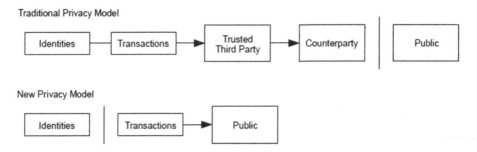

As an additional firewall, a new key pair should be used for each transaction to keep them from being linked to a common owner. Some linking is still unavoidable with multi-input transactions, which necessarily reveal that their inputs were owned by the same owner. The risk is that if the owner of a key is revealed, linking could reveal other transactions that belonged to the same owner.

Calculations

We consider the scenario of an attacker trying to generate an alternate chain faster than the honest chain. Even if this is accomplished, it does not throw the system open to arbitrary changes, such as creating value out of thin air or taking money that never belonged to the attacker. Nodes are not going to accept an invalid transaction as payment, and honest nodes will never accept a block containing them. An attacker can only try to change one of his own transactions to take back money he recently spent.

The race between the honest chain and an attacker chain can be characterized as a Binomial Random Walk. The success event is the honest chain being extended by one block, increasing its lead by +1, and the failure event is the attacker's chain being extended by one block, reducing the gap by -1.

The probability of an attacker catching up from a given deficit is analogous to a Gambler's Ruin problem. Suppose a gambler with unlimited credit starts at a deficit and plays potentially an infinite number of trials to try to reach breakeven. We can calculate the probability he ever reaches breakeven, or that an attacker ever catches up with the honest chain, as follows [8]:

> p = probability an honest node finds the next block
>
> q = probability the attacker finds the next block
>
> q_z = probability the attacker will ever catch up from z blocks behind

$$q_z = \begin{cases} 1 & \text{if } p \leq q \\ (q/p)^z & \text{if } p > q \end{cases}$$

Given our assumption that p>q, the probability drops exponentially as the number of blocks the attacker has to catch up with increases. With the odds against him, if he doesn't make a lucky lunge forward early on, his chances become vanishingly small as he falls further behind.

We now consider how long the recipient of a new transaction needs to wait before being sufficiently certain the sender can't change the transaction. We assume the sender is an attacker who wants to make the recipient believe he paid him for a while, then switch it to pay back to himself after some time has passed. The receiver will be alerted when that happens, but the sender hopes it will be too late.

The receiver generates a new key pair and gives the public key to the sender shortly before signing. This prevents the sender from preparing a chain of blocks ahead of time by working on it continuously until he is lucky enough to get far enough ahead, then executing the transaction at that moment. Once the transaction is sent, the dishonest sender starts working in secret on a parallel chain containing an alternate version of his transaction.

The recipient waits until the transaction has been added to a block and z blocks have been linked after it. He doesn't know the exact amount of progress the attacker has made, but assuming the honest blocks took the average expected time per block, the attacker's potential progress will be a Poisson distribution with expected value:

$$\lambda = z\frac{q}{p}$$

To get the probability the attacker could still catch up now, we multiply the Poisson density for each amount of progress he could have made by the probability he could catch up from that point:

$$\sum_{k=0}^{\infty} \frac{\lambda^k e^{-\lambda}}{k!} \left\{ \begin{matrix} (q/p)^{(z-k)} & if\, k \leq z \\ 1 & if\, k > z \end{matrix} \right\}$$

Rearranging to avoid summing the infinite tail of the distribution...

$$1 - \sum_{k=0}^{z} \frac{\lambda^k e^{-\lambda}}{k!} \left(1 - (q/p)^{(z-k)} \right)$$

Converting to C code...

```c
#include
double AttackerSuccessProbability(double q, int z)
{
    double p = 1.0 - q;
    double lambda = z * (q / p);
    double sum = 1.0;
    int i, k;
    for (k = 0; k <= z; k++)
    {
        double poisson = exp(-lambda);
        for (i = 1; i <= k; i++)
```

```
            poisson *= lambda / i;
        sum -= poisson * (1 - pow(q / p, z - k));
    }
    return sum;
}
```

Running some results, we can see the probability drop off exponentially with z.

```
q=0.1
z=0     P=1.0000000
z=1     P=0.2045873
z=2     P=0.0509779
z=3     P=0.0131722
z=4     P=0.0034552
z=5     P=0.0009137
z=6     P=0.0002428
z=7     P=0.0000647
z=8     P=0.0000173
z=9     P=0.0000046
z=10    P=0.0000012

q=0.3
z=0     P=1.0000000
z=5     P=0.1773523
z=10    P=0.0416605
z=15    P=0.0101008
z=20    P=0.0024804
z=25    P=0.0006132
z=30    P=0.0001522
z=35    P=0.0000379
z=40    P=0.0000095
z=45    P=0.0000024
z=50    P=0.0000006
```

Solving for P less than 0.1%...

```
P < 0.001
q=0.10    z=5
q=0.15    z=8
q=0.20    z=11
q=0.25    z=15
q=0.30    z=24
q=0.35    z=41
q=0.40    z=89
q=0.45    z=340
```

Conclusion

We have proposed a system for electronic transactions without relying on trust. We started with the usual framework of coins made from digital signatures, which provides strong control of ownership, but is incomplete without a way to prevent double-spending. To solve this, we proposed a peer-to-peer network using proof-of-work to record a public history of transactions that quickly becomes computationally impractical for an attacker to change if honest nodes control a majority of CPU power. The network is robust in its unstructured simplicity. Nodes work all at once with little coordination. They do not need to be identified, since messages are not routed to any particular place and only need to be delivered on a best effort basis. Nodes can leave and rejoin the network at will, accepting the proof-of-work chain as proof of what happened while they were gone. They vote with their CPU power, expressing their acceptance of valid blocks by working on extending them and rejecting invalid blocks by refusing to work on them. Any needed rules and incentives can be enforced with this consensus mechanism.

References

1. W. Dai, "b-money," http://www.weidai.com/
    bmoney.txt, 1998.

2. H. Massias, X.S. Avila, and J.-J. Quisquater, "Design
    of a secure timestamping service with minimal trust
    requirements," In *20th Symposium on Information
    Theory in the Benelux*, May 1999.

3. S. Haber, W.S. Stornetta, "How to time-stamp a
    digital document," In *Journal of Cryptology*, vol 3, no
    2, pages 99-111, 1991.

4. D. Bayer, S. Haber, W.S. Stornetta, "Improving the
    efficiency and reliability of digital time-stamping," In
    *Sequences II: Methods in Communication, Security
    and Computer Science*, pages 329-334, 1993.

5. S. Haber, W.S. Stornetta, "Secure names for bit-
    strings," In *Proceedings of the 4th ACM Conference
    on Computer and Communications Security*, pages
    28-35, April 1997.

6. Back, "Hashcash - a denial of service counter-
    measure," http://www.hashcash.org/papers/
    hashcash.pdf, 2002.

7. R.C. Merkle, "Protocols for public key
    cryptosystems," In *Proc. 1980 Symposium on
    Security and Privacy*, IEEE Computer Society, pages
    122-133, April 1980.

8. W. Feller, "An introduction to probability theory and
    its applications," 1957.

Index

A

Asynchronous programming, 58

B

Bitcoin spot price, 12, 13
Blockchains
    data, 30
    immutability/hashes, 30, 31
    Python, 31
        blockchain.py.code, 36–38
        class, 34–36
    Python dictionaries, 29

C

Calculations, 178, 179
Cryptographic proof, 168
Cryptography
    blockchain, 94
    digital signatures, 90–92
        verification, 88, 93, 94
    example, Python, 87, 89
    integrity, sending
        messages, 84, 85
    public key, 86

D

Decentralized networks
    Blockchain engineering,
        143, 144, 146
    funcoin
        components, 147, 148
        data persistence, 156
        networking layer, 148–156
    POS, 157
    smart contracts, 158–160
        solidicity, 160–165
Disk space, 174

E

Electronic coin, 169

F

funcoin/server.py, 141
funcoin/utils.py, 140

G

Gambler's Ruin problem, 177
Gossip protocol, 82, 150

Printed in the United States
By Bookmasters